Lesley's book will help you navi[discover who you are, what is hol[can claim true victory.

—Ka.., ~~~~~~~~, author of
Your Secret Name and *The Deeper Path*

Battlefield of the Heart reveals that the greatest challenges are within; you will be empowered to rise above all that has pushed you down. Be prepared for your heart and mind to be transformed, enabling you to live life victoriously.

—Reverend Michael K Whittle, founder and Pastor of Good News Gospel Community Church and the Amazing Charity shops in Lancashire, UK.
www.goodnewsgospel.co.uk/
www.goodnewsgospelchurch.weebly.com

Lesley is an excellent communicator who leaves a lasting impression, whether you meet her in person or read her books. She exudes joy and hope because she has found the answer to lasting contentment and peace.

Lesley has been through many battles and has found the keys to victory. In the midst of these turbulent days, it is essential that we use these keys to break out from defeat and stand tall as overcomers.

This book brings scripture to life and reveals how we can apply it practically to our lives in order to have victory on the Battlefield of the Heart.

—Andy Chadwick, Pastor at Revive Church in Stalybridge, UK.
www.revivechurch.uk

Lesley is a genuine child of God whose testimony will be worthy of note. They say that experience is the best teacher in life, and having overcome difficult times herself, she definitely can show us how to live a victorious life because we know that her testimony is built on facts and faith. Now that her "mess" has now become a message, we all must learn from her experiences in order to become overcomers ourselves. This book takes you on a journey that will liberate you from purposelessness, fear, insecurity, and other enemies of true fulfilment in life.

—Bola Akande, His Praise and Glory Media Ministry.
www.theessencetv.com
www.bolaakande.net

Lesley is an incredible person with an attitude of "never give up." She has gone through many challenges and struggles, but became strong and powerful through applying the word of God. Lesley turned to Jesus and overcame her difficult past to become victorious. This book describes how she learned to turn unpleasant circumstances into joyful situations. Battlefield of the Heart will be a blessing to everyone who reads it.

—Matthew Kurian, Pastor and public figure, co-founder of - El Shaddai Charitable Trust in Assagao, India.
www.childrescue.net

Battlefield of the Heart takes the reader on a journey of perseverance, hope, and faith. Lesley's life changed forever when she realized she had more power to take control of her thoughts and actions than she previously believed. Throughout the book, she uses experiences and bible scriptures to show the reader how they too can live a joyous and fulfilling life, regardless of past circumstances and inner turmoil.

—Diana Lynn James, author and freelance editor.
www.the-write-affair.com
https://www.facebook.com/groups/2091975234184121

BATTLEFIELD OF THE HEART

DITCH THE LIES, BELIEVE THE TRUTH, AND LIVE LIFE TO THE FULL.

LESLEY ANN WHITTLE

AUTHOR ACADEMY elite

Printed in the United States of America

Published by Author Academy Elite
PO Box 43, Powell, OH 43065
www.AuthorAcademyElite.com

Identifiers:
LCCN: 2020912634
ISBN: 978-1-64746-365-6 (paperback)
ISBN: 978-1-64746-366-3 (hardback)
ISBN: 978-1-64746-367-0 (ebook)

Available in paperback, hardback, e-book, and audiobook

All Scripture quotations, unless otherwise indicated, are taken from the Holy Bible, New International Version®, NIV®. Copyright © 1973, 1978, 1984, 2011 by Biblica, Inc.™ Used by permission of Zondervan. All rights reserved worldwide.

Scripture quotations marked (AMP) are taken from the **Amplified Bible (AMP)** Copyright © 2015 by The Lockman Foundation, La Habra, CA 90631. All rights reserved.

Scripture quotations marked (NKJV) are taken from the **New King James Version (NKJV)** Scripture taken from the New King James Version®. Copyright © 1982 by Thomas Nelson. Used by permission. All rights reserved.

Book design by Jetlaunch. Cover design by Jetlaunch.

I dedicate this book to Reverend Michael K Whittle.

All I am today is because of you. Thank you for your love, for mentoring me over the last twenty years, supporting me through all my ups and downs in life. And patiently watching me grow and develop. Love you always.

Jaqui

Live life to the full
All of Heaven is cheering
you on

Love —

Lesley Ann Whittle

TABLE OF CONTENTS

PART 3
VICTORIOUS LIVING... DEFEAT THE GIANTS

ACKNOWLEDGMENTS

A warm thank you to:

Joshua Isaac Cross, Joseph Adam Cross. Lisa Cross and Leah Lythgoe for all your support.

Thank you to all my family, and friends, for your love and making life fun.

Miss Jean Buckley, for reading through my manuscript in its earliest stages. For your helpful comments and encouragement.

Diana James, thank you for your superb editing.

Author Academy Elite, I could not have done this without you.

Thank you, Jesus, for enabling me to write this book. I pray it will be life-changing for all who read it.

PART 1

IDENTITY CRISIS... REJECT THE LIES

1

IDENTITY CRISIS

I stood at the kitchen sink with tears streaming down my face while my two boys play fight and bang around in the living room. "I can cope!" I slammed the pots into the water and looked out the window, trying to fight against the feelings of hopelessness and despair. The negative thoughts replaying endlessly in my head all day. *You can't cope because you're hopeless. Life is too difficult for you to handle.*

I was drowning in a sea of selfish negative emotions that were pulling me down. *Lord, I need your help; I am so fed up of being bombarded with negative thoughts and emotions. I can't cope. I'm useless and depressed. I'm fed up and utterly hopeless.* I didn't like myself. All of my thoughts were about me and I gave myself one hundred percent negative attention. This had gone on for as long as I could remember and I was desperate for change.

I had heard numerous teachings at church about the importance of our thoughts—we are what we think. Though I had heard this often, I had not believed it was possible to take control of my mind that way. But my thoughts were destroying me, so now, at the kitchen sink, I decided to try it out.

Starting that day I would train myself to swap every negative thought with a positive one. After I made the decision, I cried from feeling sorry for myself. Life was difficult and lonely for me as a single mum, and I had all the excuses in the world to be negative. Actually believing anything positive would be a challenge. *I'm not going down that dark tunnel again, I'm not getting depressed again, and I can cope.*

I jumped on the mini-trampoline and bounced to release those feel-good endorphins. That tunnel was pitch-black with no light waiting at the end of it. I could be down there for weeks; I would barely manage to get up in the morning to take my two boys to school. My efforts to swap every negative thought for a positive one was constant, though it took a long time to believe it was truly possible.

It was an epic battle, but I exercised to keep the depression at bay and forced myself to smile and sing. The trip through the dark tunnel got shorter each time. Eventually, I was out within a week, and then next time out in a couple of days. Soon my lonely pity parties lasted only five minutes, then even less. I was determined to change. I decided to view my time alone in the evening as a positive, and I would make the most of it by reading helpful books and my Bible. To learn, grow, and change.

Life and sanity are at the end of the dark tunnel of depression, as well as thankfulness and appreciation. I loved my boys more than ever before if that were possible. I wish I could say it was a quick transition but it wasn't—progress was slow but steady. I believed the lies in my head for years and they became deeply ingrained self-limiting beliefs. I needed to know the truth of who I truly was.

I was trapped in a victim mentality. I heard the questions so clearly in my head, always in a condescending tone saying, "Are you alright? Are you alright, Lesley?" And I would talk about all my worries, explaining in detail how I was not alright, that I felt this way and that way, or someone had said something upsetting, and I can't do this or that ... you get the picture. By the time the conversation was over, I not only felt worse but even sorrier for myself than before.

When I realised the truth, I was furious with the Devil. God never asked me, "Are you alright?" in such a pitying voice. Never! And He doesn't want us throwing pity parties or feeling sorry for ourselves; He never intended for us to be victims in life. In Jesus Christ we are not victims, we are victors. We are transformed by His power and we can live a victorious life.

Victims say, "Poor me, all the world is against me. It's all right for you because you haven't experienced what I've been through." Your past does not have to determine your future. You are not what your past experiences say or what your neighbour says—you are what God says you are.

The trouble with a victim mentality is that it's addictive. You love the sympathy, you crave the attention—it may be the only attention you get. But this mentality is manipulative. Your behaviour might cause people to walk on eggshells around you, which could potentially make you take offense and add them to your list of people who have "done you wrong." Your perception becomes convoluted and you can no longer see reality. You have to kick yourself and make the decision to no longer feel sorry for yourself.

I thought about how I got to this point in my life. I didn't know who I was anymore—I had lost my identity somewhere along the way. "For what purpose have I been placed on planet Earth?" As I thought less about myself and more about others, I realized I wasn't alone in feeling this way. Many people I met had experienced an identity crisis during their lives and no longer knew who they were supposed to be. They had believed the lies and had nothing good to say about themselves. They were held back from making any real, lasting progress in life because of their false beliefs.

From where did these negative thoughts and limiting beliefs originate? They certainly did not come from God; all of His thoughts towards us are positive, creative and forward-looking.

Jeremiah 29:11 says, "'For I know the plans I have for you,' declares the Lord, 'plans to prosper you and not to harm you, plans to give you hope and a future.'"

When people speak negatively about you, or you speak negatively about yourself, darkness reigns. We can speak life or death, blessings or curses. These are in the power of the tongue because there is power in what we confess. Proverbs 18:21 (AMP) states, "Death and life are in the power of the tongue, and those who love it and indulge it will eat its fruit and bear the consequences of their words."

We have to stop and ask ourselves what our thoughts are focused on. Catch your negative thinking, analyse it, then change your thought process. Have a serious and strengthening self-talk based on God's word. He knows you're a wonderful person, so be positive and start believing it too. If you do not line up your thinking with what God believes about you, this means you are disagreeing with the potter who moulded the clay. You cannot get very far in life if you are at war with God and His word.

The first lie ever told was spoken in the Garden of Eden by the "father of lies", Satan himself. John 8:44 says, "For he is a liar and the father of lies." Satan is the originator of deceit. In Genesis 3:1-5 we read, 'Now the serpent was more crafty than any of the wild animals the Lord God had made. He said to the woman, "Did God really say, 'You must not eat from any tree in the garden?'"

DID GOD REALLY SAY?! Satan sows seeds of doubt in your mind so you waver in your decisions and find yourself questioning your own beliefs. "You must not eat from ANY tree in the garden." Satan distorts what God has said by twisting the truth to make it sound believable. We read, "The woman said to the serpent, "We may eat fruit from the trees in the garden, but God did say, 'You must not eat fruit from the tree that is in the middle of the garden, and you must not touch it, or you will die.'"

"You will not certainly die," the serpent said to the woman. "For God knows that when you eat from it your eyes will be opened, and you will be like God, knowing good and evil."

AND YOU WILL BE LIKE GOD. Eve was already "like God" because she was made in His image, as are each one of us. We lost our true identities, but they will become clearer as we look to the one who created us and read his instruction manual for a blessed and prosperous life. As we read God's word and journey with Him, we will discover more about who we are and why we are on planet Earth. We are works in progress and there will always be room for change and improvement. When we have children, we love them unconditionally, including any faults or failings, as they learn and develop. Our Heavenly Father loves us in the same way.

Satan is the original identity thief and has always twisted the truth; he has not changed his tactics and he never will. He wants us to think we are missing out on something, that God is withholding something from us. He wants us to believe that bad things happen to us because we are displeasing to God and that we are not worthy of approaching God in prayer to ask for what we need.

Satan's job description is, and always will be, "to steal, and to kill and to destroy," according to John 10:10. He does not want us to discover who we really are or God's amazing plans for our lives. He desires us to be trapped by lies, never able to fulfil our destinies. He will try anything to contaminate our faith with fear and keep us bound in unbelief and low self-worth. He loves to hear us say, "I can't do that," and "I'm not good enough," or "Everyone else can do it better than me."

As long as we believe these lies, he has us right where he wants us—unable to move forward and reach our goals and potential. We are not useless, we are not incapable, and we are not rubbish; we've believed his lies for too long. Once we accept one of Satan's lies, he will take advantage and pile on loads more. If we reject his first lie and then his second, he sees we will not take the bait and will leave us until a more opportune time.

Satan is the great accuser and he will use the mouths of humans if he can to criticise you, belittle you, and fill your head with negativity. The Devil has no voice on the Earth so he uses people who will agree with him to be his mouthpiece. He loves taking you on guilt trips, reminding you of all your failings. But God is love and He sent His son Jesus to die on the cross for all our sins, to cleanse us. We can walk tall knowing we are cleansed by the blood of Jesus. 1John 1:9 says, "If we confess our sins, he is faithful and just and will forgive us our sins and purify us from all unrighteousness."

God speaks words that give life, light, hope, healing, love, and blessings. He speaks empowering faith-filled words over us, and we need to do the same. We need to believe who God says we are and all that Jesus did for us on the cross. We must know that we can fulfil our dreams and that we can be confident in the awesome power of our God. No matter what heartaches we have faced in the past, healing begins inside our hearts and minds.

I spent so long trying to fix the outside by attempting to change my life and improve myself with my actions, just to feel happier and better about myself and be accepted by others. The truth is that nothing external can alter the value God has placed on us. We are unique and priceless to Him. Jesus didn't die on the cross so I could make improvements to my life for the approval of others. He died that I might live a victorious, abundant, eternal life! What we are on the inside is displayed on the outside. We have His very life, His nature, and His abilities inside each of us. A great seed of potential is within.

We need to have faith in what Jesus has already made possible, to believe what he believes, and to speak what he would speak. We have a choice and it starts with our thinking. You can't have negative and positive thoughts simultaneously. You can't think highly of someone at the same time as thinking badly about them.

Imagine you are on an aeroplane and you want to use the toilet, but you can't get in because it's occupied. You can't just barge in. You have to wait for a vacancy, and it is the same with your mind. You need a sign in your head that says "occupied." While your mind is fixed on what is good, no other thought can barge in. When you are determined to praise and thank God, the devil cannot bombard your mind. You can't sing praises while sitting with your head in your hands listening to negativity and worrying about life. You need to occupy your brain with positive thoughts.

When I realised I could actually control my thinking, my life changed completely. I had believed my thoughts dictated who I was, oblivious to the fact that I could choose to think differently. I did not have to sit down, head in hands, thinking about all my worries. I could choose to think positive thoughts, read books and the bible, or listen to an encouraging podcast. I could thank God out loud for the small things I didn't realize I could be grateful for until I made the conscious effort to do so.

Being thankful changed my whole outlook on life—my thoughts, my speech, and my feelings. I could finally smile and feel a little happiness. It takes time, but we can change what we think, and more importantly, what we believe about ourselves. It is a process because we have been programmed to think a certain way for such a long time.

As children of God, we can reprogram our minds to think like our Heavenly Father. Romans 12:2 tells us, "Do not conform to the pattern of this world, but be transformed by the renewing of your mind. Then you will be able to test and approve what God's will is—his good, pleasing and perfect will."

When we read the Bible, our minds, and therefore our lives, are renewed and transformed. We are reading God's thoughts and witnessing His character. We begin to think as He does by having thoughts of blessings instead of curses, and opportunities as opposed to defeat. We then speak life-changing words of love and power, and our nature becomes more like our Heavenly Father's. We become more caring, humble, and thoughtful of others. We understand and live for what is truly important. Reading the bible changes lives—it is the very word of God.

Many young children believe what you tell them without question. As God's children, we believe what we hear, and what we constantly hear, we eventually believe. We are responsible for what we fill our minds with and what we choose to read and listen to.

Words can run on repeat in our heads and our lives are governed by these thoughts. We can never be greater than what we think or how we speak. We only experience things by what we choose to think and say; we cannot go somewhere we have never thought about. The more we read God's word, the more our lives will change for the better. We will be able to see ourselves as God sees us.

Invest in yourself by spending time with the Word and take time to discover who you are so you can live out God's plan for your life. You can only give out what you put in, so don't pull yourself down by believing the lies. Celebrate that you are on a life-changing journey. Enjoy the process of transformation; don't waste another day being miserable and fed up. When you enjoy your day, those around you can enjoy the day as well.

You can't be in two places at once—you are not fully living out your day while your head is somewhere else, be it focused on the past or on a problem. Rejoice in the truth that Jesus loves you and is working with you to identify the Devil's deceptions. Jesus wants to replace the lies with the truth of who you really are according to God our Creator. The thoughts we have about ourselves must be based only on what God thinks about us, not our own opinion or the opinions of others.

The way you view yourself is the way others will see you. Your opinion of yourself is more important than what other people think of you, whether great or small. We must not live to fulfil the expectations others have of us because when we do that, we are not living our own lives to the full. If you are constantly trying to better yourself in your own strength, you will end up feeling like a failure, never measuring up regardless of how well you do. You will go through life limping and pulling others down with you.

You must learn to like yourself, accept where you currently are in life, and give yourself time and space to grow. Live your life to the full, and follow your dreams. The Bible says to love others as you love yourself, so you cannot love others and give freely unless you love yourself.

God loves us completely and approves of us unconditionally, not just because of what we have or have not done. He could never love us more or less than He does at this very moment. He breathed his very life-breath into us and we are very special to Him. We have believed for too long that our value is placed on what we can achieve. Our true value is in our identity and in Jesus, to whom we belong.

"For you created my inmost being; you knit me together in my mother's womb. I praise you because I am fearfully and wonderfully made; your works are wonderful, I know that full well. My frame was not hidden from you when I was made in the secret place, when I was woven together in the depths of the earth. Your eyes saw my unformed body; all the days ordained for me were written in your book before one of them came to be. How precious to me are your thoughts God! How vast is the sum of them! Were I to count them, they would outnumber the grains of sand—when I awake, I am still with you." Psalm 139:13-18

2

AM I ENOUGH?

Am I pretty enough? Am I clever enough? Am I strong enough? Am I doing enough and accomplishing enough?

I always thought everyone else was better than me. I wanted to be the best, or at least as good as others. It didn't matter what I was trying to do; I always felt inadequate, ineffective, insignificant, and pushed aside. I desired to be accepted and liked.

These feelings began with a specific incident in my childhood. It was a lovely sunny day and I was happy while collecting all my favourite teddy bears, as many as I could carry. Off I ran, across the road and into my friend's back garden, where the teddy bear picnic was about to begin. Jackie and I arranged the blankets, the plastic cups and plates, a few bags of crisps and a bottle of raspberry juice. We had a lovely time, but it wasn't long before Sarah arrived.

Immediately, Jackie turned to me and said, "You can go home now, you have to go home!" I disappointedly grabbed all my favourite teddies, interrupting them from their picnic. "You can leave your teddies here and get them later," Jackie piped up.

"What!" I thought. The cheek of it. There was no way I was going to leave them there.

This early incident was the first of many in my life, introducing me to a stream of rejection and of feeling insignificant. I always put myself down and caused myself pain because I expected not to be liked. I knew people would always have a poor opinion of me, so I had a very poor opinion of myself.

Suffering endless rejection in life can be stifling, but the more we forgive those who rejected us or mistreated us, the more developed our healing process will be. I have learnt I need to pray blessings on people, not to curse them. We also need to bless our own lives by being careful about what we think and say about ourselves. Our thoughts and words are seeds that have the power to produce life or death, victory or defeat, happiness or misery.

It is easy to compare ourselves with others and think they have no problems. Perhaps they are more attractive, are always smiling and happy, have better jobs and can afford holidays. Or we think they are more organized or popular, and that they have everything going for them.

The way I stopped myself from this excruciating exercise in jealousy and self-doubt was to ask myself, "Would I swap my life with this person—have their job, their friends, the whole package? Or do I like my life better?" I would have to be willing to swap every aspect of our lives, even if they did not have a relationship with God. I was satisfied to say, "No, thank you." I am thankful to God for my family, my job, the place he has given me to live and my companions in life.

I decided to repeat to myself, "Someone else's success does not take away from mine. Someone else's attractiveness does not take away from mine. I am one of a kind. If God loves me, why shouldn't I love myself? He has a great plan for my life." Celebrate your uniqueness and the uniqueness of others. You are the only you there is, so be the best and happiest you that you can be.

In my head, I knew that God loved me for who I was, but in my heart, I wasn't so sure. I always wanted to do more, to be more and to achieve more because I felt I was never good enough. I fell short no matter what I did. My expectations of myself were too high, and I let myself down constantly. I never reached the expectations of people in the past, so I was regularly seeking the approval I could never get before.

One day I realized I might never gain that elusive acceptance and I had to stop living solely to gain the approval of others. I needed to learn to like myself as I am. By not focusing on accomplishments for the sake of recognition, I could, instead, try to find the real me so I could be free.

Our loving heavenly father has created us uniquely and loves us as such. He wants us to be able to say, "I'm free to be me!" I desperately wanted to be free to be me, but I didn't know who that was anymore. Who was I supposed to be? How should I think and feel, and what do I truly believe? What was I passionate about? What was my purpose and what did I want to do with my life?

I had so many questions and no answers, leaving me empty and numb. I had stopped dreaming and hoping long ago and had completely lost myself. I needed to find out who I was. When I finally realized that God loved me simply for being me, I lay down all the negative thoughts, worries, and concerns about my life and future every time they arose. I concentrated on the moment and making small decisions to build upon. I quit striving only to please, seeking to be liked, desiring to be loved, and started my life over again.

When we feel we are not enough, we can draw close to the one who *is* more than enough. We are already loveable and important. To try to become what we already are causes unnecessary frustration and stress. We do not need to accomplish tasks for God to love us; He loved us before we were born and before we achieved anything. As noted in Romans 5:8, Jesus died for us on the cross while we were still sinners and at our worst. Once we are secure in His love, love itself will drive us; we will live and be and do out of the love in our hearts and for the right reasons. Love must be the foundation we build our lives upon.

God is love. When we rest and relax in His love, and when we accept His love into our hearts, we can begin to love ourselves. We will feel loved and feel accepted, and therefore we can give love and care to others in return. When we are in severe pain, all we are able to do is focus on ourselves in a negative way; this is not living, but only existing. By reaching out and helping others, we find our purpose and find happiness in something that is bigger and more meaningful than ourselves. Helping others is a wonderful way to discover who you are.

I have learnt that the most important thing I can do is to be me—to relax and be true to who I am in this moment, knowing God's love towards me. Instead of seeing myself as being the most important and dominant person in my thoughts, I can focus on genuinely loving, encouraging, and helping others. If you are not sure what to do first, be helpful. I've found so much joy in being thankful and helpful, and it can also help you discover where you fit.

A friend of mine once told me a story. He was sat for hours praying in the church hall when the pastor finally came out of his office and asked, "Michael, What are you doing? You have been sat here all morning."

"I'm waiting to hear from God," he replied.

"Umm… well!" said the Pastor. "Meanwhile, here's the mop and bucket." In other words, he was saying that while you are waiting to hear from God for direction, listen to others and be helpful. He also pointed out the importance of obeying the "him" who you can see. If you can't obey the "him" you can see, how can you obey the "Him" who you can't see? If you are in doubt of what to do or you can't remember the last instruction He gave, be helpful and you can't go far wrong.

It is important to recognize that the reason we are alive is more important than our own dreams and fulfilment. That would be too small a purpose. God has a much bigger plan for us than we can imagine. Jeremiah 29:11 says, "For I know the plans I have for you, declares the Lord."

God desires that we live a meaningful, purposeful and abundant life. John 10:10 states, "I have come that you may have life and life to the full." When you help others, God will help you. It is like seedtime and harvest—we reap what we sow. As Mike Murdock says, "What you make happen for others, God will make happen for you."

It is true that what we feed, grows. So instead of focusing on our weaknesses or problems, we can focus on others and all that is good, giving a fine report. If we constantly feed a poor self-image of ourselves, focusing on our weaknesses and failings, we will find ourselves in darkness. What you begin to starve will die, but if you fuel your life with good thoughts, your confidence will grow. Feed on the truth of God's word, pray and declare it out loud over your life, then keep repeating the process until you can smile about it, believe it, and walk tall.

Reading God's word is vital. We can meditate on what we read by asking ourselves questions. For example, "who am I in the story?", "Am I the one needing help or the one helping?", and "What can I learn here or what example can I follow?" The more we read about Jesus, the more we will understand our true identity. We will discover the difference between our old nature and our new nature, as God intended.

When we are weak, then we are strong. There is nothing wrong with having weaknesses because it is then that God's strength can work through us. Less of us and more of him. He can reveal his glory through our weaknesses more than through our strengths. Our pain and struggles of the past can help set others free. In 2 Corinthians 12:9-10 it states, "But he said to me, "My grace is sufficient for you, for my power is made perfect in weakness. Therefore I will boast all the more gladly about my weaknesses, so that Christ's power may rest on me. That is why, for Christ's sake, I delight in weaknesses, in insults, in hardships, in persecutions, in difficulties. For when I am weak, then I am strong."

What you feed will grow and what you starve will die. Practice focusing on loving others and God's love for you. When you know you are loved by God, you are free to focus on others instead of yourself. You are confident your needs will be provided for and everything will work out all right. As we digest God's food, we automatically change for the better and will become a stronger, happier, fulfilled person. We can discover and develop a strong foundation of who we are and become more secure in ourselves.

My insecurity was the foundation my life was built upon. All that I thought was true was destroyed and all I stood upon was taken out from beneath my feet. I was unstable, but in a way, it wasn't a bad place to be. It gave me the opportunity for a new foundation and new truths to stand upon in belief. My life was sinking in the sand; I felt I had lost everything. But it became a brand new start.

Edward Mote wrote a famous hymn in 1834. "My hope is built on nothing less than Jesus Christ my righteousness" The chorus reads, "On Christ the solid rock I stand, all other ground is sinking sand." The words are so true and powerful that we still sing it today. The more we know who Jesus is, the more we will understand who we are. But if our hopes, security, and foundations are elsewhere, we could collapse into the sinking sand.

I had a dream: I was a rose that had been trampled on the ground and all my petals were squashed and damaged. I closed up and became introverted. My petals were weak and fragile, tightly pulled in. My Heavenly Father, the gardener, who I only knew as God, took hold of me and placed me in a special garden where he could take care of me. He fed me, watered me, and strengthened me internally. One by one, my petals opened up, ever so slowly. I needed a lot of healing in my heart and mind. It took a long time before I felt and looked like a beautiful, confident rose in full bloom.

Our Father will not leave us as He found us; He loves us too much for that. It is more painful to grow than to give up in defeat. But our Father takes care of us, prunes us and heals our life, making it meaningful and fulfilled. He gives us a future and a destiny. He calls us as his own and cherishes us.

"Am I enough?" In a way, I can say that no, I am never enough, but that is a good place to be—dependant on He who is more than enough. I can never get to heaven based on anything that I do because we were all born through the same sinful bloodline. I can never be worthy of God's grace by my actions. I am worthy only by the blood of Jesus. He took my unworthiness with him on the cross and in its place gave me his righteousness.

"Am I enough?" In a way, I can say that yes, I am enough, because I have received the love and acceptance of the King and creator of the universe. Jesus is the great 'I AM' and his presence and power lives in us by his Holy Spirit. You can be confident that no matter what God asks you to do, He will equip you with everything you need to succeed. He sees from the beginning to the end and knows both where He wants you and how to get you there. Wherever you are in life right now, remember that each day counts. The choices you make today impact your tomorrow. Take one day at a time. Do your best—nothing more and nothing less.

PART 2

IDENTITY REVEALED...
Believe the Truth

3

MORE THAN ENOUGH

J esus is more than enough and whatever your need may be, the provision can be found in him. He is above all things and created all things. There is no name higher than the name of Jesus—his name is higher than depression and higher than any sickness. He is King of Kings and Lord of Lords; his word is above every other opinion. We can go to his word as our utmost and final authority in our lives, for every situation we find ourselves in. His powerful spoken word created the universe and is higher and more powerful than the physical evidence we see with our natural eyes.

God said, "Let there be light," and it was so. We are His children made in His likeness, with the same creative power by the words we confess, whether positive or negative. Scientifically, bodies respond to the thoughts running through our minds. Our lives line up with our words and this is an awesome astonishing power. God knew what He was doing with His intricate design.

In Matthew 9:18-19, 23-26 we read, "While he was saying this, a synagogue leader came and knelt before him and said, "My daughter has just died. But come and put your hand on her, and she will live." Jesus got up and went with him, and so did his disciples. When Jesus entered the synagogue leader's house and saw the noisy crowd and people playing pipes, he said, "Go away. The girl is not dead but asleep." But they laughed at him. After the crowd had been put outside, he went in, took the girl by the hand, and she got up. News of this spread through all that region." Jesus threw everyone out of the room—all the doubters, all the unbelievers, and all those who displayed negative behaviour. He cleared the room so a miracle could take place in an atmosphere of faith.

My pastor was preaching this story one day in church and I saw myself in that room Jesus was in. I thought *doubt out and unbelief out, get out of the room of my mind.* I needed a new brain, a new way of thinking. I had become negative at work, negative about my friends, negative about my life—everything was viewed with negativity.

By swapping every negative thought and belief with a positive one, I was replacing my thoughts with the words of God, renewing my mind, and changing the outcome of my life. We must clear our mind's room of all the unbelief, negativity, and doubt. Our minds can be invaded by all sorts of thoughts and we need to clear it so all remains are truth and the most important things.

2 Corinthians 10:5 says, "We demolish arguments and every pretension that sets itself up against the knowledge of God, and we take captive every thought to make it obedient to Christ." What does this mean? Some think God's word is foolish or out of date, but there is more wisdom in it than in the entire world. We decide we will believe and act upon God's word as truth to demolish our own arguments against His word.

Philippians 4:8 says, "Finally, brothers and sisters, whatever is true, whatever is noble, whatever is right, whatever is pure, whatever is lovely, whatever is admirable—if anything is excellent or praiseworthy—think about such things. Whatever you have learned or received or heard from me, or seen in me—put it into practice. And the God of peace will be with you."

I've taken a long journey already, but I continue to intentionally practice taking every thought captive to the obedience of Christ. A few years back, I stood in the charity shop where I worked, feeling sorry for myself. All I could see were problems and the mess around me, yet I felt powerless to change things. I was negative and tried to solve the problems by myself. I didn't know where to begin and had to come to the point of total helplessness and surrender.

I said, "Lord, if you help me and show me what to do, then I can do it." From that day forward, my thoughts and attitude changed, and as they did, so did everything else. Jesus is more than enough—when I got to the point of defeat, he stepped in to help me. When we feel what we do is insufficient, we can surrender to the one who is more than enough.

When negativity and darkness come and we feel sorry for ourselves, we cannot see the truth. We forget all the good we have done. I had forgotten I was changing people's lives—the people I have met, shared with, and prayed with. I helped build a school and water wells with the funds we've raised. I was part of something bigger than myself and something more than one person alone could do. My impact and input as a part of a team are valuable and so is yours. When we think right, we can see right.

If I arrive at work and I am not all right in my thoughts, attitude or emotions, I become critical of everything and everybody else. But if I am all right, I'm happy, bright and optimistic with a positive view of everything and everybody else. The day and the people aren't different, nor is the environment or situation different. The difference is me and my positive point of view.

The mundane daily routine of life makes us who we are and causes us to mature and develop. In a film called "The Karate Kid," a young boy named Daniel wanted to learn karate, so he asked an old Chinese man, Mr. Miyagi, to teach him. Mr. Miyagi had the boy perform tasks that seemed irrelevant to him. He instructed Daniel to drop his coat, pick it up, then hang it up over and over and over. Daniel then had to clean Mr. Miyagi's old car while the old man repeated, "Wax on, wax off, wax on, wax off." And repeat, and repeat, and repeat. Daniel finally had enough and walked off.

"Come here Daniel," called Mr. Miyagi. Daniel stood in front of Mr. Miyagi who asked the boy to repeat the movements one more time, but with no coat and no car. As he did so, Mr. Miyagi blocked Daniel's moves, who then realized he had learned karate all along, using everyday movements he was familiar with.

We sometimes wish life to be more exciting and adventurous than it presently is, instead of living our daily routine on repeat. God uses this to build character. He is always preparing us for what's next, even when your job is to put beans on the shelf, repeat, repeat, repeat or wash clothes and hang them up, repeat, repeat, repeat. Repeat with joy, faithfulness, and everything you have within you because it is a planned setup. God is getting you ready for what is next. Daniel did not fight in public until he had practiced in private. Even when no one is looking, do your best with the best attitude you have. You are making an impact on your future.

After nearly quitting, Daniel realized the movements he was performing—the ones he viewed as small and insignificant—were powerful. His training began at "ground zero" with no prior knowledge or experience. Everyday actions we see as small or insignificant point us to our success through the school of life. Our attitudes and willing obedience prepare us for the future. We can up and run, leaving our responsibilities behind because we find them too difficult and boring, or we can stop complaining and faithfully get to work.

It is easy to think, "Surely this isn't God's plan for my life, I want to do something great!" We can't see ahead, but God, the master of the universe who created us as His masterpiece, has a more awesome plan than we can imagine. We must not give up, but every day walk in love and take advantage of the opportunities He gives to bless the One and add to the One, in front of us. If we can't love and bless the One, how will we ever be able to love and bless the multitudes?

When we feel we are not enough, we must say, "That's ok, because I am in the hands of the one who is more than enough. He lives in me and can work His purposes in me and through me." All He needs is a humble, surrendered vessel to work through. We can be His hands, His feet, and His mouthpiece.

Jesus is working on us, inside and out, whether or not you are aware of it. Keep faithful and do your best, even when you know no human is looking because God sees all and is preparing you. He is about to promote you, so what you are doing right now is no mistake. God has called on you to be wherever he has strategically placed you at this moment in time. Ask him to show you the impact you are having on people's lives right where you are, and to show you how you are a blessing to the people you meet and serve. You are changing lives.

We are not just passing time, trying to find something to do to fill a gap between now and the future we hope for—we are now. We are to faithfully concentrate on being grounded and rooted in love. The greatest change in our lives is inside our hearts, which then spills out to impact others. Jesus called us as we were, so with his help we are more than enough to accomplish what he has planned. We have the power and the boldness of the Holy Spirit within us. The bible says we are more than just conquerors at Romans 8:37.

He also gives us a personal responsibility to grow. If we continually eat junk food, we feel ill, but if we eat well-balanced diets, our bodies know. It is the same with our spirit. I once heard the phrase, "Invest in yourself because you will get one hundred and ten percent harvest." At first I viewed this as a selfish statement. *Are we not supposed to invest in other people's lives and the Kingdom of God?* But as I thought about this, I realized it was true. We can only give out what we put in; we can only give away what we have possession of. If we continually feed on good spiritual food, it will spill out of our hearts when needed to change someone else's life.

You are a life-changer. You have the power and the word of God within you—His life, His nature, and His ability. Simply start with the person in front of you. As you love people and serve them, you will be amazed at the opportunities God provides. Jesus said the greatest among us is he that serves. To go up you must go further down and find ways you can serve, no matter how insignificant it seems. Your life and what you do with it is a gift of love to Him who gave you life.

If you are anything like me, you wanted to become someone important with a life of true meaning, born for a reason and not simply for existence. You already are this person. When I tried to become who I already was in God's eyes, I was full of frustration, unhappiness, and self-preoccupation. The greatest thing we can do to offer the greatest love we can give is to be a willing sacrifice to Jesus and serve him as King.

How do we serve him? Matthew 25:37-40 says, "Then the righteous will answer him, 'Lord, when did we see you hungry and feed you, or thirsty and give you something to drink? When did we see you a stranger and invite you in, or needing clothes and clothe you? When did we see you sick, or in prison and go to visit you?' The King will reply, 'Truly I tell you, whatever you did for one of the least of these brothers and sisters of mine, you did for me.'"

What we do unto others, we do unto him. Jesus is not physically here on the earth, so you serve others as his ambassador. What an awesome privilege! Jesus called the disciples to follow him and imitate what he did. He has likewise called on us be his followers and increasingly become more like him.

My Pastor has a funny saying, "Jesus could not be here with you today, so he has sent me!" It's true—Jesus is in Heaven and he has commissioned us to be his representatives on this Earth. The good news is we are not alone because he has sent his Holy Spirit to help. Believe that God's almighty power is at work in you. He handpicked you and He believes in you. Be bold and declare who you are; don't sit listening to the enemy and the storms around you, but sing praise. His love is more powerful than any enemy, even death. Jesus was willing to sacrifice his very life for us; his love conquered and defeated death on the cross.

God's love for us is more powerful than anything that comes our way. His love is more powerful than hate and human emotions, more powerful than sickness and death. God's love casts out all fear and anxiety. What is there to be afraid of? Perhaps you fear not being enough, displeasing to God, or unable to fulfil your calling?

When you were a child at school, you may not have been picked for the netball or football team, but God has picked you to be in His family. Who can compare with God? No one. There is none higher, yet we are chosen for His team and He provides for us. Nobody tells Him what to do; He chooses us and draws us close because He loves us. When would I need to be afraid of what other people think or say about me when I am chosen by God? What does it matter what people may feel or believe? When you know who you are and who Jesus is, you won't care what other people think of you.

When you are confident that Jesus will meet all your needs, you can relax, love him, and worship him. Then you will discover what he wants you to do to reach out and bless other people. Don't keep the secret to yourself—share Jesus with others. We were all made to have a loving relationship with him.

When Jesus died on the cross, it wasn't to improve us, fix us, or patch us up. He didn't come into our lives only to fill in the cracks and smooth us over. Imagine a large wall in your home that you want to decorate has many cracks and holes in it; some are huge while others are tiny fractures. You fill them in with a suitable decorator's filler, pressing it into the crevices and smoothing it out. Eventually, you may cover everything with wallpaper so you can no longer see the repairs. But you know the cracks were there, the big holes were there, and though they have been repaired, the wall underneath will never be rid of its repaired damages.

That wall is a prime example of my life, but for a long time, I couldn't fill the big holes in my life or heal the cracks and fractures. I was broken. Jesus came into my life and he fixed me, but he did not fill me in or patch me up. He took down the entire wall and foundation. He rebuilt me on a firm foundation, brick by brick, as a newly plastered wall. After all, he created me and loved me enough to not leave me in the state that I was in, though I wasn't fully aware of his presence or love. It didn't happen overnight—I had to willingly cooperate. It took a long time to heal and become the person I am today.

Jesus did the same for you. He did away with the old wall inside and made you brand new. 2Corinthians 5:17 shows, "Therefore, if anyone is in Christ, the new creation has come: The old has gone, the new is come." You are restored, forgiven, and purposeful. Healing is a process and we have to play our part in it. We need to learn to forgive and to let go of the past and all that would hinder us. We must also overcome any disappointments about how we thought life would turn out. Healing takes time, but we can help the process along by speaking as if we have already arrived. When you feel inadequate, say, "I can do all things, Lord, because you strengthen me." We should view ourselves whole and have the same viewpoint of ourselves as our loving Heavenly Father does.

We can search the whole world through and not find any help for our secret suffering and shame. Some would rather go through life carrying their heavy load and wandering around aimlessly with a constant limp than surrender and submit to our creator. They are often afraid of what he might request from them because they think, "How can he love me?" Most of us like to be in control of our own lives and to be our own bosses. Do we think we can make a better job of it in life than Jesus can?

Jesus is our saviour, our healer, and our creator. If we will surrender to his love and healing process and submit to his ways, we may suffer some discomfort, but it will be worth it and we will be amazed what he can do in our lives. When we struggle to do what is right, Jesus is more than enough. When we feel tense, Jesus is more than enough. When we are weak, he is our strength. His grace is more than sufficient for us in times of need. He is more than enough and that is not dependent on anything we do or don't do.

In Matthew 14:15-21 we read, "As evening approached, the disciples came to him and said, "This is a remote place, and it's already getting late. Send the crowds away, so they can go to the villages and buy themselves some food." Jesus replied, "They do not need to go away. You give them something to eat.""We have here only five loaves of bread and two fish," they answered. "Bring them here to me," he said. And he directed the people to sit down on the grass. Taking the five loaves and the two fish and looking up to heaven, he gave thanks and broke the loaves. Then he gave them to the disciples, and the disciples gave them to the people. They all ate and were satisfied, and the disciples picked up twelve basketfuls of broken pieces left over. The number of those who ate was about five thousand men, besides women and children."

Jesus had compassion for the crowd; he saw they were physically hungry but more than that, they were spiritually hungry. Jesus fed them both physically and spiritually through this miracle and revealed to the people that he was more than enough. Jesus prayed over the food and gave thanks. He didn't multiply the food to be just enough, but more than enough. He is not going to help you just enough for you to get by or keep you going. He is so much more than enough that if you allow him to be your source, you will never need for anything outside of his provision.

Jesus longs to provide for you; he is jealous for you. He wants to shower his goodness on you to overflowing abundance so that you will not be a person of 'enough to get by', but a person of 'more than enough'. Abundant in love, in joy, and in all things so that you may be a blessing to others so they will see God's goodness for themselves. Never doubt that God can do far more than we could ever imagine.

4

IDENTITY REVEALED

"As Jesus was walking beside the Sea of Galilee, he saw two brothers, Simon called Peter and his brother Andrew. They were casting a net into the lake, for they were fishermen. "Come, follow me," Jesus said, "and I will make you fishers of men." At once they left their nets and followed him." (Matthew 4:18-20.)

In John 1:42, it says that Andrew, Simon's brother, introduced him to Jesus, and as soon as Jesus laid eyes on Simon for the first time, he said to him, "You are Simon son of John. You will be called Cephas"—which is translated as Peter. Jesus saw Peter at his best, though he was at his worst. He saw the potential for who Peter would be in the future with his developed character. Jesus sees you and he knows you inside and out; he sees you at your best and knows your future.

Simon Peter was a Jewish family man who lived by the Sea of Galilee and had a fishing business with his partners. Jesus called, "Come follow me," and Simon Peter, along with the others, followed. They heard Jesus preaching, "Repent, the Kingdom of Heaven is near." To follow means to "come after; pursue; go along; to copy; obey; adopt opinion; watch fixedly; to focus the mind on and to gain understanding." Jesus must have made a significant impact on Simon and the others for them to leave their fishing business. They saw an opportunity of a lifetime—the privilege to follow this teacher called Jesus.

At once, they lay down their nets and followed him. They lay down their business, their agenda, and let go of the past. They put aside their lives as they knew them to have a new beginning with the one who was the Way, the Truth and the Life. They knew only what they had heard from others about Jesus. They did not yet understand their new purposes in life, but they were hungry and teachable. Being humbled by the troubles of life provided an opportunity for Jesus to pour his all into them.

Simon was about to embark on a wonderful life-changing journey. He needed no intelligence or character tests; Jesus called him as he was, not because of any special skill he might have. Jesus said to the disciples, "I will make you fishers of men." After a busy day of fishing, the disciples would be hungry and need to eat. But now they would hunger for a different type of fish—the souls of men. They were to lay out nets filled with the enticing bait of the life-changing, good news of Jesus. We have what the world hungers for. We carry the life-changing, eternal good news of the Way, the Truth and the Life.

You may be a highly sought after adviser or a professor at the top of your field, but when Jesus says, "Come follow me," and you accept him as your Lord and Saviour, you start at ground zero. With Jesus, we all begin our journey knowing nothing. You will soon discover who you truly are is likely not who you thought you were. You have a new heart and a new identity; you enter a new kingdom with new rules, so you need to renew your mind. You will let go of your life as you knew it and release the past to receive an amazing and purposeful future.

When Jesus first met Peter, his name was 'Simon', which means "reed"—blown and tossed about by the wind, unstable, a wavering one. Jesus gave Simon a new name, calling him "Peter" which means "rock"—steady and stable, strong and reliable. Not only does Jesus give Peter a new name, but also a new identity and a glimpse of his future, giving him a purpose for living. (Matthew 16:18) No longer was Peter to be known as a wavering one, but a rock who would help build the church. Jesus had said to Peter, "Feed my sheep." (John 21.) God gives us the hope of a great future; he shows us a glimpse of what is to come and gives us new visions and identities.

In Matthew16:13-18 we read, "When Jesus came to the region of Caesarea Philippi, he asked his disciples, "Who do people say the Son of Man is?" They replied, "Some say John the Baptist; others say Elijah; and still others, Jeremiah or one of the prophets." "But what about you?" he asked. "Who do you say I am?" Simon Peter answered, "You are the Messiah, the Son of the living God." Simon had received a revelation from Heaven about who Jesus was. Jesus then decided to reveal to 'Simon son of Jonah' his true identity as Peter the rock and a glimpse of his future. Jesus replied, "Blessed are you, Simon son of Jonah, for this was not revealed to you by flesh and blood, but by my Father in heaven. And I tell you that you are Peter, and on this rock I will build my church and the gates of hades will not overcome it."

As Peter followed Jesus and witnessed the miracles performed, he discovered Jesus was love in action. Jesus even visited Peter's home and healed his mother-in-law. Peter became close to Jesus, one of his inner circle of three. The time came when Peter was sent out along with the other disciples and they were given authority to heal the sick and cast out demons. This was before Peter was perfect and before much-needed character development.

When we look at Peter's character, we see that he was unstable initially. He was rough around the edges and had little grace, frequently making mistakes. He often spoke without thinking, which got him into trouble, but on the positive side, he was not afraid to make decisions or take action.

Peter, like you and me, had many ups and downs. In Matthew 16, after Peter receives revelation of who Jesus is, he becomes proud and ends up rebuking Jesus. In verse 21-23, Jesus explains to his disciples that he must suffer many things, be put to death, then on the third day be raised to life. "Peter took him aside and began to rebuke him. "Never, Lord!" he said. "This shall never happen to you!" Jesus turned and said to Peter, "Get behind me, Satan! You are a stumbling block to me; you do not have in mind the concerns of God, but merely human concerns."

In chapter 18 we see Peter asking how many times he must forgive others. He had been finding this difficult to do and wanted to justify himself. In Matthew 26, Peter says to Jesus, "Even if all fall away on account of you, I never will." Jesus replied, "Truly I tell you, this very night, before the rooster crows, you will disown me three times." But Peter declared, "Even if I have to die with you, I will never disown you," and the other disciples said the same. Poor Peter did deny Jesus three times that night and wept bitterly. This is the same Peter who later suffered persecution, who was put in prison, and eventually was crucified on a cross because he refused to deny Jesus—he became a changed man.

After Peter denied Jesus, he needed to be reinstated and restored. In John 21:15-17, Jesus asks Peter a question three times. "Peter do you love me?" "Yes, Lord," he said, "you know that I love you." Jesus said, "Feed my sheep." Peter was reinstated into his rightful place and identity. Jesus did not need to know the answer to the question, Peter did. Our love for Jesus means we are willing to let mistakes, troubles, and the daily routine of life help us develop a godly character.

In the book of Acts, we see Peter boldly preaching—what an amazing journey he had. Peter became a completely different man. When the lame man at the temple in Acts 3 got up and walked, Peter let everyone know he had nothing to do with it and it was only by the power and the name of Jesus. Peter became a respectful, submissive, and humble man. When we read his letters in first and second Peter, we see how his character developed and how he learnt a great deal.

In 2 Peter 1:5-8, he talks about moral excellence, self-control, perseverance, godliness and brotherly kindness. He did not always fully live up to these character traits, but he grew and developed. This gives hope to us all. For as long as we are alive on planet Earth we have not made it yet and we still have a lot to learn. We will never stop becoming more like Jesus as we continually choose to love him, follow him, and serve him by fulfilling our calling. 1 Peter 2:9 says, "But you are a chosen people, a royal priesthood, a holy nation, a people belonging to God, that you may declare the praises of him who called you out of darkness into his wonderful light." Peter knew who he was, and this applies to you too.

God had an amazing plan for those disciples and He has an amazing plan for you. Once you believe, you can succeed; you will give your all, for God has designed you to be a success. If you believe in what you are called to do, you will give it all you've got, and when you believe in Jesus, you become fully committed. Like Peter, you will have many adventures and may, from time to time, get it wrong. But the most important thing you can do is stick close to Jesus, being sure of his love and plan for your life. He loves you and believes in you.

Satan is the great identity thief and does not want you to know or believe the reality of who you are, because if you learn the truth, there will be no stopping you. Believe the truth of who you are and who God says you are because He knows and sees your potential. He supports you and can help you change your life around if you believe in His word and His principles above any other. In a world full of opinions, renew your mind by the word of God and adopt His viewpoint; this is what was meant when Jesus said, "Come follow me."

The more we read God's word and understand who Jesus is, the more we will learn who we are. When we read the word of God, we can see ourselves in the lives of Bible characters as though we were looking into a mirror and his word washes us clean. We can uncover our true identities when we align our words, actions, characters, and attitude with the word of God.

We can also see that Jesus sees us at our best. He sees us victorious, as our end products. God is outside of time and sees our beginnings, our middles, and our ends simultaneously, as if looking down at a traffic jam from a helicopter; you can see the entire scene from start to finish. But when you are in the middle of a traffic jam, all you can see is your current situation. You can't see what is up ahead, but God knows all of your tomorrows.

The most important things you can do in life are spending time with Jesus and reading his word. The disciples spent a long time with Jesus and later they watched him ascend into Heaven. We see in Acts 4:13 that the elders and teachers of the law were astonished when they discovered the disciples were unschooled, ordinary men with great courage. We often become like those who we spend the most time with and Jesus' influence on the men was noticeable. They thought as he did, spoke as he did, and even performed miracles as he did. You too will do even greater things than this, but surrendering to his influence is the key. Give in to his plan and the work he is doing inside you, and surrender to his word when you are tempted to do things your own way.

God knows the potential he has placed within you and you will bear much fruit as you continually walk with Him because He has filled you with His Holy Spirit. He calls you faithful and strong; He calls you a fisher of men before you ever see it in yourself. He sees your true identity and how you will grow and mature into it before you realize He is talking about you. He knows your uniqueness and gifting, He sees your hearts desires. Your true identity is only found in Jesus—in who he says you are and what he says you can do in this world. He who created you has placed a calling within you; he places dreams and desires in your heart by the Holy Spirit at work in you so that you may fulfil your destiny.

This is your identity; you were bought with a price, so you are no longer your own. You belong to the Father and He has commissioned you. He does not want us to keep the good news a secret, but to share it with the world. If you do not know what to do in life, start by being helpful and serving others. Love and help the person in front of you. Using your personality and talents, your love will grow and be a witness for Jesus.

You are an undefeated, victorious champion. You have faith, hope, love and good news on your lips. You were designed for success; whatever you put your hand to will prosper. You were designed to be free—free from past mistakes, free from oppression, free from fear and from worry. You are free to live abundantly and free to be you.

We need to believe in ourselves and that we were born on this Earth for such a time as this. We can be life-changers in our generation; we can make an eternal difference.

5

CONSTANT, STEADY AND STABLE

"Shortly before dawn Jesus went out to them, walking on the lake. When the disciples saw him walking on the lake, they were terrified. "It's a ghost," they said, and cried out in fear. But Jesus immediately said to them: "Take courage! It is I, don't be afraid." "Lord, if it's you," Peter replied, "tell me to come to you on the water." "Come," he said. Then Peter got down out of the boat, walked on the water and came toward Jesus. But when he saw the wind, he was afraid and, beginning to sink, cried out, "Lord, save me!" Immediately Jesus reached out his hand and caught him. "You of little faith," he said, "why did you doubt?" Matthew 14:25-31.

Here we see Jesus walking on the water; Peter steps out onto the water and walks towards Jesus. While Peter kept his eyes on Jesus, who is love, he did not sink. But as soon as he took his eyes off of Jesus' "love" and looked at the severity of the fierce storm surrounding him, he became afraid and sunk. Perfect love casts out all fear; as we keep looking to Jesus as our rock, we will not be afraid and we will not sink. In life there will always be storms; we need to believe more in the abilities of God than we do of the storms and of what our eyes can see. We need to have "stickability" when the going gets tough. Keep going and never give up because all of heaven is cheering you on.

We place our faith and our beliefs firmly on Jesus Christ. He is the steadfast, immovable rock on which we stand—all other ground is simply sinking sand. We have a choice to trust in Jesus, the King of Kings and Lord of Lords, and his word more than we trust what we see with our natural eyes. To doubt is to be uncertain of God's ability to help you through, and to believe that if he *can* help you, does he really *want* to help? "Why would he want to help me? Does he really care? Does God really love me?"

As a child, I once pulled the petals from a flower and chanted, "he loves me, he loves me not," until there were no more petals to pull. We need to believe above all else that God's love for us is not like the petals of a flower; it is forever, constant, strong, and immovable. If we doubt his love for us, we doubt everything else. Love is a powerful force that runs through us. When we love our bodies, we take care of them and keep them strong because what we love is precious to us.

When we are aware of God's love, our pain melts away like sunshine thawing snow. His love pours upon us and we are full of his peace. His love melts the hardest hearts, but if we don't believe, then we won't be able to receive it. What you believe in your mind will affect your body, your health, the directions you take, and everything else in your life. Remember, when you doubt, you sink, just as Peter sank in the water.

In the previous chapter, we looked at Simon, whose name means a wavering "reed"; one minute he believed and the next minute he was in doubt. He was unsteady and unstable, as his name implied. James 1:6-8 tells us, "But when you ask, you must believe and not doubt, because the one who doubts is like a wave of the sea, blown and tossed by the wind. That person should not expect to receive anything from the Lord. Such a person is double-minded and unstable in all they do."

Simon was double-minded and tossed to and fro. He was boisterous, arrogant, and made many mistakes. But when he met Jesus, everything changed—his name, character, attitude, speech, and his purpose. His whole life changed from the inside, out. As Peter, he was a steady, stable rock, immovable and unshakeable. He became a devoted follower of Jesus, a preacher and a teacher, a humble, willing, obedient servant, and disciple of the Lord preaching the gospel of Jesus Christ and turning the world upside down.

The only one way we can remain constant, steady and stable is by standing upon the rock. Jesus is that rock on which we are to stand—we are to rely upon him, feed upon him, love him, serve him, and fellowship with him, to become rooted and grounded in him. He is our confidence and our strength. If we decide to go our own way, we will sink. 1 Peter 2:4-10 tells us that Jesus is the living stone, and when we trust in him and rely upon him, we will never be put to shame or be disappointed.

Colossians 2:6-7 says, "So then, just as you received Christ Jesus as Lord, continue to live your lives in him, rooted and built up in him, strengthened in the faith as you were taught, and overflowing with thankfulness." Build up your faith by staying connected to Jesus. Read his word, sing his praises, and have an attitude of thankfulness. Being thankful will strengthen your belief and the more you believe, the more you will be thankful.

We can become constant, steady and stable by having a close and personal relationship with Jesus. Not only knowing *about* him, but truly knowing him *intimately*. We must have close and personal relationships with him every moment of the day, not just when we have a problem. We can have a close connection with our heavenly Father by thanking him, loving him, and being aware of his existence and his presence, as he intended when he created Adam and Eve.

When we are troubled, we can silently pray, "Lord, please keep me constant, steady and stable." Constant in that we don't change who we are because we have a difficult day. Steady in that we take our time and don't get flustered or stressed. And stable in that we remain reliable. Our emotions can get knocked about or come under attack, so we need God's help to remain constant, steady and stable. Jesus is the rock on which we must stand.

In John 15 we read that Jesus is the true vine and we are the connecting branches. The vine and the branches have the same sap running through them, the same life and love. Everything Jesus has, we have, as we remain connected to him. Verse 4 says, "Remain in me, as I also remain in you. No branch can bear fruit by itself; it must remain in the vine. Neither can you bear fruit unless you remain in me." His love and power can flow through us to touch this generation. We are one with him and share the same purpose.

Think for a moment of your closest companion, perhaps a spouse or a close friend with whom you can talk openly and freely, and laugh or cry. You can share private details with one another because of the trust you have developed between you. My friend will make me a cup of tea and see to my needs without me asking because he already knows my preferences and what I need. This friend brings me gifts from time to time, like bouquets of beautiful flowers. He provides advice and helps me develop new ideas. We love each other's company and desire to be together. We don't need constant conversation in order to enjoy each other's company because we feel near and connected. This is how it is with Jesus; he is your closest companion.

We don't come to Jesus with a list of demands and concerns and then just walk away. He has already promised to care for us and desires, above all else, our fellowship with him. We pray and ask for what we need as the Bible instructs, but that is not all that is expected. Even when we are grumpy, we can still spend time with our heavenly friend as this time can strengthen us and bring us joy. We don't have to wait until we feel more sorted out to come to him because we feel unworthy. Be with him and his presence will be with us no matter what our moods may be. We need not fear rejection; his love for us is so powerful that he can settle us and enable us to be constant, steady and stable.

As we let the words of our mouths change our lives, our attitudes, and our directions, we can become more constant, steady and stable. Even a small rudder on a ship can direct and control the whole vessel because it cuts through the water. Your words can cut through the atmosphere and steer you the right way. Let Jesus be the captain of your ship; speak his words and obey his instructions.

Your attitude is crucial. When you go through a storm, be it immense and life-altering or small, like when someone tries to ruffle your feathers, stay where you are and stay peaceful. Don't let the storm or other troubles on the outside get inside of you. Keep your peace; let your character, your whole nature, remain steady. When you let your emotions stay calm and even, you can choose your responses carefully. If you try but fail, draw close to Jesus and he will sort you out again.

In life, we can be unsettled, inconsistent, and fickle, but by trusting in Jesus we can keep steady through the storms and adventures of life. His love for us is constant and immovable; he is our firm foundation. We can steady ourselves by agreeing with God and following his word. We can steady ourselves by what we tell ourselves and what we choose to believe. To focus and stabilize our lives, we must focus and stabilize our minds.

2Corinthians 1:25 says, "It is by faith you stand firm." Faith is believing that all will turn out well, even when the situation appears disastrous, and thanking and praising God for a miracle before it happens. Faith is being immovable against any negative thoughts that appear and any lies that our enemy, the Devil, tells you. His job is to kill, steal and destroy. Be fixed upon God's word as sovereign in your life.

There is a man in the Bible who was given an unfortunate name. He was called Jabez and his name meant "pain." Wherever he went he became a pain to others, but he also experienced many pains in his own life. With great determination to not live up to his name, he pursued a blessed course. He turned his life around with strong, bold prayers, and the words of his mouth.

1Chronicles 4:8-10 reads, "Jabez was more honourable than his brothers. His mother had named him Jabez, saying, 'I gave birth to him in pain.' Jabez cried out to the God of Israel, 'Oh, that you would bless me and enlarge my territory! Let your hand be with me, and keep me from harm so that I will be free from pain.' And God granted his request."

In life, you may have been handed an unfortunate start. But your past, your upbringing, your name or reputation, and even your life circumstances, do not have to dictate your future. You can choose to overcome these obstacles and change your misfortune into fortune; change your misery into joy and your weakness into strength. You can achieve this by knowing, trusting and standing upon the immovable rock, Jesus Christ, our Lord. Put his teachings into practice by standing on his word, believing in his word, declaring his word into the atmosphere, and offering bold prayers. It is when words are released into the atmosphere that they manifest in the physical world. God spoke into the atmosphere, "Let there be light," and it came to be.

We read in Matthew 7:24-26, "Therefore everyone who hears these words of mine and puts them into practice is like a wise man who built his house on the rock. The rain came down, the streams rose, and the winds blew and beat against that house; yet it did not fall, because it had its foundation on the rock. But everyone who hears these words of mine and does not put them into practice is like a foolish man who built his house on sand. The rain came down, the streams rose, and the winds blew and beat against that house, and it fell with a great crash."

When we put the words of the bible into practice, we are acting wisely—building our houses and our lives upon the rock, Jesus Christ. We will not fall flat when the storms of life rage against us and when the enemy pours in like a flood. We shall stand firm and strong. We become stronger and more stable as we are constant with God's word in our lives; over time, we develop our faith if we continually exercise it. Likewise, our physical muscles don't appear after only one session at the gym. When we have stored up God's word in our heart, it becomes our nature. What is on the inside of our hearts is displayed on the outside by our words and actions, and the Holy Spirit will bring it out from our memories when we need it.

When we feel unsteady and unsure, when circumstances make us wobble at the core of our foundations, and when our confidence falters due to unpleasant situations, we need to ask ourselves, "What am I believing for? What am I telling myself? What am I worrying about?" Anxiety and depression come from what our mind dwells on because what we focus on is magnified. If we think of something funny our child said, we will laugh, pushing out negative feelings. We cannot think happy thoughts and sad thoughts at the same time. We must dwell on what is good and secure, not on problems or thoughts that bring instability and insecurity. Tell yourself it *will* be all right.

6

LOVE BEYOND MEASURE

In 1 Corinthians 13:1-8 and verse 13 we read, "If I speak in the tongues of men or of angels, but do not have love, I am only a resounding gong or a clanging cymbal. If I have the gift of prophecy and can fathom all mysteries and all knowledge, and if I have a faith that can move mountains, but do not have love, I am nothing. If I give all I possess to the poor and give over my body to hardship that I may boast, but do not have love, I gain nothing.

Love is patient, love is kind. It does not envy, it does not boast, it is not proud. It does not dishonour others, it is not self-seeking, it is not easily angered, it keeps no record of wrongs. Love does not delight in evil but rejoices with the truth. It always protects, always trusts, always hopes, always perseveres. Love never fails. And now these three remain: faith, hope and love. But the greatest of these is love."

Jesus is patient and kind, but most of all, Jesus is love. Love is the most important gift we could ever receive and 1 Corinthians 13 encourages us to desire and pursue the path of love. Imagine I bought a nicely wrapped gift but I mean-inglessly shove it into your hands and say to you, "Here, have this gift I bought you." It is given with no love, kindness, or care. It means nothing; you would feel better not receiving the gift at all. In life, the most important quality we can possess is not spiritual gifts nor any earthly treasure, but love. We can lay hands on the sick or preach the gospel but if we have no love, we are making a loud, terrible and useless noise. Emptiness is all we have.

People are crying out for love and acceptance, yet so many reject the love that is Jesus. There is no greater love than that which Jesus gives, a love that lays down his life that you may live. John 15:13 shows us, "Greater love has no one than this: to lay down one's life for one's friends." Love is not wishy-washy, nor is it weakness, nor saying what you know people want to hear. Love is truth; "You shall know the truth and the truth shall set you free," John 8:32.

Love shouts near danger and snatches from the fire. Love is not a feeling, but an act of your will. Sometimes you feel love or affection and sometimes you don't, but that doesn't mean love has vanished. The question is, what will love cause us to sacrifice for that person, with or without the feelings? Would we sacrifice time, money, or our own desire? Would we sacrifice our life? Are we willing to be patient and kind even after we have worked all day and feel we have given our all?

We are drawn to what we love—we spend time doing what we love and we serve it. We were created by love himself and were designed to love God and other people in return, as well as to have the desire to be loved. Love is the perfect environment for a happy, healthy, productive and fulfilling life. It is like sunshine and the very air we breathe; it heals our bones and revitalizes our whole being. Love keeps us alive with passion and purpose.

If we don't know we are loved, we will yearn for it. People are so desperate for love that they search for it in all the wrong places; human nature craves more and more and is never content, never fully satisfied in its search for love. We may not realize we are loved because we have false perceptions and don't know what true love looks or sounds like.

Love is protective and sacrificial, it's giving your life and pouring out your all. We were created to worship based on our love, and if we don't worship God we will worship someone or something else because of our nature. Love changes you—it changes how you feel, think and operate. Love changes how you live; you live with purpose, passion, and hope.

In the workplace, we will thrive. We will do our best, hit our targets, and we will enjoy our work. If we hate what we are doing, or just find work unpleasant, we lose our sense of purpose and die on the inside. I have found that if I *choose* to enjoy doing something, I will enjoy it. It all has to do with who we are, not where we are or what we are doing. I can be the best me wherever I am and in whatever I am doing, taking pleasure in the challenges and opportunities that arise. I can enjoy and grow with the people I work with; what you tell yourself and the attitude you decide to have makes all the difference.

Sometimes love means doing what you find challenging in order to bless others. The workplace became a difficult place for me and I felt like giving up, though I wouldn't have in actuality. I realized my attitude was the biggest problem, but changing my attitude was not easy. I chose to be thankful for the job that God had given me. When I am all right on the inside, everything on the outside follows suit.

We were created by love himself—we are his most treasured, beautiful, prized creation. We can have the most intimate fellowship with our heavenly father as Adam and Eve had in the beginning. Satan is on a mission to snatch God's children away, tempting us and leading us away from the truth. He feeds us with nothing but lies; he wants us to think we are missing out on the truth and fun in life.

If God tells us we can't have something, it is because he is protecting us. He knows it will harm us and he wants only the best for us. God has not hidden any truths or any good thing from us, rather he hides it for us to find. The Bible says in Matthew 7:7 to seek and you shall find. At John 14:6, Jesus tells us, "I am the way and the *truth* and the life. No one comes to the Father except through me."

The Devil snatched us away, but we were rescued again by love—love that would not leave us behind and would do anything to restore what was lost. A love that would leave his home in heaven and become human to die on a cross. He suffered the painful death that we deserved for every sin we have committed or ever will commit. 1 John 3:16 says, "This is how we know what love is: Jesus Christ laid down his life for us. And we ought to lay down our lives for our brothers and sisters."

After God's creation obeyed Satan in the garden, how could we ever fellowship with our Father again? God had a plan; love finds a way even when there seems to be no way. The day came when God said to his son in heaven, "It is time!" He came down to the earth, spent nine months in a human womb, and put on flesh to dwell amongst us as we see in John 1:14.

The greatest love story ever told—God sent his son to die for us in order that we could be restored to him and have the intimacy he had with Adam and Eve in the garden, the highest form of pure intimacy. Jesus paid an awful price—he died that we might live and he rose again. He conquered death, he conquered sin for you and me, and he reigns victorious. Love is powerful and gives all there is to give, pouring out his life for us.

Jesus' love is everlasting—he doesn't switch on and switch off on a whim. Love is not a feeling, but an act of your will. Sometimes you may feel love and sometimes you may not, but God's love is constant and eternal, and he has put his love in our hearts as described in Romans 5:5. We have the ability to love with the love of God within us.

There are four types of love: "Eros" is sensual or romantic love, "storge" is family love, "philia" is brotherly love that unites believers, and "agape" is God's love for humankind.

This fourth type of love is immeasurable and incomparable; it is perfect, unconditional, sacrificial, and pure. John 3:16 says, "For God so loved the world that he gave his one and only Son, that whoever believes in him shall not perish but have eternal life." If you want to know what "love" looks like, take a look at "love" himself. Jesus is our perfect example and his love enters our hearts by his Holy Spirit when we accept him as our Lord and saviour.

In Ephesians 3:17-21, Paul prays for the Ephesians because he wants them to understand how much they are loved. And as they are rooted and grounded in love, they will be strengthened in their inner being and in their thinking. Believe that God can do immeasurably more than we can imagine. "So that Christ may dwell in your hearts through faith. And I pray that you, being rooted and established in love, may have power, together with all the Lord's holy people, to grasp how wide and long and high and deep is the love of Christ, and to know this love that surpasses knowledge—that you may be filled to the measure of all the fullness of God. Now to him who is able to do immeasurably more than all we ask or imagine, according to his power that is at work within us, to him be glory in the church and in Christ Jesus throughout all generations, forever and ever! Amen."

Below are the words of a song I wrote to play on the guitar. I was inspired by Psalm 103 and am grateful for God's amazing love and care for me. He rescued me from darkness and from the pit of hell. He reached down, took hold of my hand and pulled me out, then brought me into His marvellous kingdom of light. I am in awe of His goodness and love for me and will never be the same.

"You rescued me from darkness; you crowned my life with love. You fill my life with good things, you're so good. So merciful and gracious, you forgave me all my sin. You set my feet upon a rock and gave me life again.

Bless the Lord o my soul, affectionately praise. All that is within me Lord bless your holy name. O bless the Lord o my soul, affectionately praise. All that is within me Lord bless your holy name.

I will sing a song of praise to you, with all my heart I worship you, I will sing a song of praise to you, with all my heart I worship you. Forevermore I adore you.

I'm in awe of your goodness; I'm in awe of your love. Jesus, you have saved me, by your precious blood. I bow my knee before you; I sing a song of love. Forever I'm so grateful for the things you've done."

When you are sure of Jesus' love for you, you will want to repent and turn away from all those things that Jesus died on the cross for. When you receive and know God's unconditional love for you, this truth will set you free to love God, love yourself, and love others. You will no longer feel the need to prove yourself because doing so won't make him love you more. He loves you completely.

You don't need to be in competition with others who you feel are more successful, attractive or popular. You can relax in his love, smile, and say, "I am free to be me." Your walk with him is unique. His love for you cannot be measured and cannot run dry—it is like an ever-flowing river of life.

The Devil, the Great Accuser, will try to keep us away from God's love, as shown in Revelation 12:10. He loves to make us feel unworthy, unable to run into God's loving arms because of the mistakes we have made. Our intimacy with Jesus is the key. When we look at the Psalms, we see David was openly honest and talked to God about everything, then he declared, "Yet, I will praise the Lord."

David was named as a man after God's own heart. He made big mistakes, but he repented and continued to fellowship with God. There is a difference between getting everything right and to be in right standing with God. We can be honest, keep short accounts, repent and praise the Lord for what he has done for us on the cross, and enjoy his love and presence. Whatever mess you make, God can help you out of it. As you continue to grow with him, the severity of your mistakes will decrease.

God has a great plan for your life, so he will put you alongside the right people who can sand the rough edges from you. It's easy walking in love while you're at home alone, but when you get into the crowd, your love is put to the test like gold in the furnace being purified by the fire. Tests and trials are good for our character development and promote us to the next level God has for us.

If you never did another good thing, God would still love you. For years, I did not realise I was trying to earn God's love. In my head, I knew God loved me but deep down I never felt good enough and always pushed myself to achieve more, to be more productive. Accomplishments made me feel good about myself.

One day, I woke to realize he simply loves me for me. Yes, I will grow and develop, yes, I will change because of his power at work in my life, yes, I will do great things and reach many with the gospel, but this makes no difference to my intimacy with him. He desires me for me, not what I can do for him. I can enjoy life being with him, and the rest is the fruit from that intimacy. Let love beyond measure flow through you.

7

GREAT EXPECTATIONS

D o you get up in the morning and dread the day? Do you hit snooze on the alarm, turn over and go back to sleep? This is your day to shine! You only get this day once before it's gone forever, so make the most of it—make a big splash, make an impact, be a life-changer. Choose to say, "This is the day the Lord has made, I will rejoice and be glad in it." Remember that you can choose your attitude. Tell yourself, "Come on, soul. Rejoice, smile, and enjoy the day." You may have gotten up late, or the sky may look dark in general, but Jesus is the same yesterday, today and forever. If Jesus is in your boat with you, be certain all will be well.

I woke up one day and realized I'd lost my sparkle. Everything was going well—I was happy, encouraging to everyone, and didn't have a bad word to say about anyone. I enjoyed my work, even singing throughout the day. I was usually purposeful and full of positive energy, but that day was different. Where had the sparkle gone? I felt flat as a pancake; I had lost all sense of joy and purpose.

It is great when your feelings are your friends, but you cannot rely on them. If we allow our feelings to take charge of our days and lives, all of our decisions would be based upon them and we could spoil our friendships and our productivity.

If we realize we can still control our emotions when we don't feel "on top of the world," we can create our day with a positive, faith-filled, bible-believing confession.

"Thank you, Lord—I am expecting a great day today. I know you are with me and we will do well together. I thank you that your presence is with me. I believe and trust in you. I choose to rejoice and be glad so I can remain steady through whatever tries to pull me down." I remember a song from long ago by Don Francisco that went something like, "Praise the Lord Hallelu, I don't care what the Devil's gonna do, my word and faith is my sword and shield, Jesus is the Lord if the way I feel."

Each day only comes once, so you should live it to the full. Be an overcomer of obstacles, take control of your thoughts, reign over your emotions, sing, and sparkle. I find my joy rises when I sing; when I have the joy of the Lord, I then have strength. As Nehemiah 8:10 says, "The joy of the Lord is my strength."

So even during great adversity, even if you wake up feeling as flat as a pancake for no reason at all, you can have great expectations because God is still the same. God desires for you to have high expectations because when you do, He can do something wonderful. He is happy with your faith as shown in the scripture, "Without faith, it is impossible to please God."

One day when I read this, I realized God's emotions are not as constant and as still as I thought. He can be pleased on a deeper level when we have faith. I imagined Him grinning at me because of my trust and my expectations. I see faith and expectation as chariots that God can ride upon to act on our behalf. Faith is being sure of what we do not see and having total confidence in God and His word.

Have high expectations in life and believe in the greatness of now and that the best is yet to come. Speak over your life, sing and rejoice. The Devil's job has not changed—he is still the Great Deceiver. He will tell you not to bother getting up today because nothing exciting will happen. He wants to spoil your day before it has begun. But the power of God hasn't changed either. In the morning, when you wake up say, "Thank you, Lord. I'm expecting a great day. I'm expecting your favour upon my life. I'm expecting successful sales. I thank you, Lord, in advance. I thank you for all your goodness." When you lay your head on the pillow at night, you can say, "Thank you, Lord, for a great day. I'm expecting a lovely refreshing sleep."

God's great love for us is fixed and unchangeable. His presence is constant—He doesn't come and go. We learn how to stay in His presence, and to constantly be aware of His presence with us. If a friend has been constant in life, they have been with you for a while and have shown their loyalty. We can expect the promises of God's word to be continuous, unbroken and everlasting in our lives. His love and healing regularly flow over you like a waterfall. He never runs out of faithfulness does not have a short supply of anything. Philippians 4:19 tells us, "And my God will supply every need of yours according to his riches in glory in Christ Jesus." We can expect He will provide for us and meet our every need."

We can dip our toes in the river of life or we can jump in and be saturated. The choice is ours but the supply is constant. I wrote a song about the river of life, Jesus, and how there is joy, peace, and continual healing to be found there. There are wisdom and victory in the river of life—all we need can be found there. We can expect that God will communicate with us. "Call to me and I will answer you, and will tell you great and hidden things that you have not known," says Jeremiah 33:3.

As we look ahead in life, we can choose what to expect. We can imagine a bleak unfulfilled future or we can envision many positive things like wisdom from God, salvation in our families, growth in our churches, and we can foresee all of God's promises to come to pass. He will guide us by the Holy

Spirit, providing refreshment and abundant life. He will pour His anointing upon us to do His work.

Pray in expectation of a great church service or a great day at work. Be confident that your situation will get better. Expect God to speak to you and the Holy Spirit to guide you. Know that your relationships will get better, your life will get better, and your attitude will get better. Expect miracles.

I once made a big mistake in my kitchen. I had three layers of old flooring and instead of laying new flooring on top of the bottom layer, I began pulling it up. It was a big job and I had only made it halfway through when things went downhill. Everything was a total mess and the floor needed to be without lumps and bumps. The sticky glue was affecting my chest, making me unwell. I felt sorry for myself because of the mess I had made. I was extremely repentant for having made myself a lot of unnecessary work and asked God to give me ideas to make the job easier, as well as the will to continue. I felt like giving up, but leaving it in that state wasn't an option.

I went to church that Sunday and the message preached was, "Don't give up on God; he never gives up on you." I thought, "This was so encouraging. God hasn't given up on me so I shouldn't give up either. When I make a mess, I am not to give up on myself, my dreams or the task at hand. When I looked at the problem I had created, I felt overwhelmed and fed up with myself, but I decided I must expect the wonderful lovely outcome. This kept me going. When we make foolish mistakes, we can learn from them, repent, and trust in God's love and grace. We can expect His help.

Expectations in life can work for or against us, depending on whether we have high or low expectations and good or bad expectations. But when our expectations are in God and His word, we are thinking in line with the creator of the universe, our heavenly Father. We can look to Him and trust Him to fulfil the promises He gave us in His word. Our expectations in Him will always be met because God will always do exactly what He says He will. Joshua 21:45 says, "Not one of all the Lord's good promises to Israel failed; every one was fulfilled." If our expectations are not in line with God's word and promises or His character, we could end up being disappointed because He doesn't act the way we think He should or line up with our requests. His thoughts and ways are much higher than ours.

I love Ephesians 3:20 because it says, "Now to him who is able to do far more abundantly than all that we ask or think, according to the power at work within us." We are to ask big and dream big. Though what we are asking seems big to us, it is tiny to God. There is nothing too difficult for Him. Our expectations of God are always too small because He is so big compared to our human experiences.

God is miraculous; He brightens and transforms your life. Though life can be difficult, Jesus lifts you above the storm so you can walk on the water. My pastor says, "Don't let the storm on the outside get on the inside." With Jesus in your boat, the boat of life, you will be alright and get through the tribulations. You will arrive on the other side.

Always expect Jesus to show up for you and always expect the best. When going through a storm, I like to remember that, "This too will pass." Expect to come out stronger. When you expect the best, you want to thank God for His goodness. You sing because you are truly certain of His love, His power, His ability, and His divine plan. You know your breakthrough is on its way, so you can rejoice before you see the outcome.

I often speak to people who are anticipating the worst to happen. I might say, "Hi, what a nice day," and they reply, "Oh, it won't last long. It will probably rain later." Or I could say, "Much success at the job interview," and the reply is, "Oh I don't think I'll get it. I never do." They are so used to being disappointed that they disappoint themselves first, so no one else can. I was the same way—I wouldn't get my hopes up because I believed they would be dashed. Nothing good ever happened to me and I thought that was just the way life was.

I was without hope for a better life. If I asked for anything, I just knew I'd be turned down. I expected others to dislike me and reject my ideas. Because I led my life that way, I got exactly what I expected. That was how life went until my mind was renewed by the good teachings of God's word at church, and until I saw God's love and goodness through other people. I was disappointed in life for a long time. Disappointment is the big gap between your current situation and your dream.

People often expect the worst to happen because of previous experiences, but we attract what we confess. If you could have what you confess, what would your confession be? God's word is powerful, so if you vocally birth his word over your life into the atmosphere, you are giving your thoughts tangible life. Keep watering your seed by speaking that confession until you can see the evidence with your eyes.

When I decided that life was bigger than me, I was able to overcome most disappointments. There were other people out there with real problems, yet they didn't whine and moan as I did. They helped other people and seemed happy doing so. When I began to leave myself aside and helped others instead, the seed that had been planted grew and I changed.

As Mike Murdock says, "What you make happen for others, God will make happen for you." If you need healing, pray for someone else to be healed, doing so with love and not just to benefit yourself. If you have financial difficulties, bless someone else who is in need. When you lose your self-importance, you will gain your life in return. You will find life is good when you make other people's lives better. Don't hold on to your own life, especially if it has been difficult. You may as well focus on improving someone else's life, and then you can expect your life to improve as well.

Jesus is faithful in completing the work he began in you, as shown in Philippians 1:6. This is proof that you will reach what God has designed for you. He loves you unconditionally as you are, but His great love for you always has better things ahead—He won't leave you where you currently stand. Your faith will grow deeper and your effectiveness for the gospel will be greater. If God is for you and pleased with you, who can be against you? He will work with you on your attitude, your ability to take instructions, and will help you be joyfully helpful, even when you don't feel like it. He will work with you on the dreams that He has put in your heart.

PART 3

VICTORIOUS LIVING... DEFEAT THE GIANTS

8

THE GREATEST BATTLE

In chapters 13 and 14 in the book of Numbers, we read the story of Moses sending out the twelve spies to Canaan. He told them to spy the land and bring back a report. Chapter 13 verses 17-20 says, "When Moses sent them to explore Canaan, he said, "Go up through the Negev and on into the hill country. See what the land is like and whether the people who live there are strong or weak, few or many. What kind of land do they live in? Is it good or bad? What kind of towns do they live in? Are they unwalled or fortified? How is the soil? Is it fertile or poor? Are there trees in it or not? Do your best to bring back some of the fruit of the land." So, they left with enthusiasm on their mission to spy the land.

When forty days passed, they returned home to give a report of what they had seen. Ten of the spies came back with negative reports, which they spread among the people like wildfire. They reported, "We cannot attack those people, they are stronger than we are! There are giants in the land, we can't do it. We seemed like grasshoppers in our own eyes, and we looked the same to them."

They were defeated even before they had begun; defeated by the confession of their mouth and the spreading fear of the people. They looked at the giants and the challenges before them and melted in fear like wax. Their opinions of themselves were small, and so they looked small in everyone else's eyes because of the confessions of their mouths.

A bad report and complaining will get you nowhere. You won't defeat anything by complaining, worrying, or being afraid. All you will achieve is defeat, and all before you have a chance to start.

Likewise, you can be a champion before you begin. Only two of the spies, Joshua and Caleb, came back with a good report. When they saw the giants they may have been tempted to run away, but their focus was not on the giants, the problems, or what their eyes could see. They were steadfast to what the Lord God had promised them. They ignored any feelings of fear and trusted in the almighty, powerful living God who parted the Red Sea and rescued them from Pharaoh and the Egyptians. A good report magnifies the goodness God and is a way of faithfully declaring the victory before you see the outcome. A good report strengthens you on the inside and makes you stand tall as though anything was possible.

In chapter 14, verses 7-9, Joshua and Caleb reported, "The land we passed through and explored is exceedingly good. If the Lord is pleased with us, he will lead us into that land, a land flowing with milk and honey, and will give it to us. Only do not rebel against the Lord. And do not be afraid of the people of the land, because we will devour them. Their protection is gone, but the Lord is with us. Do not be afraid of them."

God promised the land to them long ago. In Exodus 3:7-8, The Lord said, "I have indeed seen the misery of my people in Egypt. I have heard them crying out because of their slave drivers, and I am concerned about their suffering. So I have come down to rescue them from the hand of the Egyptians and to bring them up out of that land into a good and spacious land, a land flowing with milk and honey." Victory was absolute.

Did these two men not see the giants? Did they spy a different land? Not at all. They knew God promised to give them the land and they believed in His promises. Victory was certain, they knew they would defeat the giants, though they couldn't just walk in without a struggle. You may think your greatest battle is what you see on the outside, but it is actually the battle we face on the inside—on the battlefield of the heart. We have to win the fights in our minds and hearts before we can win against outside challenges. Joshua and Caleb won the battle over fear, so they were able to accomplish what they set out to do.

I believed fear served as a warning sign that stopped me from moving forward because I would fail. "Don't do it—I'm not good enough and I don't know enough. It's not God's will." Fear steals your faith. Fear will paralyze you and force you back into your previous ways, having never broken through the gate towards victory. I was deceived for years. I discovered that the greater the level of fear, the greater the threat the Devil must be feeling. He desperately wants to stop you from achieving your purpose.

When I am afraid, I try to remember that it is, as 2 Timothy 1:7 (NKJV) describes, a spirit that comes upon you, that certainly isn't from God. "For God has not given us a spirit of fear, but of power and of love and of a sound mind." You can defeat the giant of fear by realizing that the fear does not belong to you—it is Satan's fear and it comes for you, but you do not have to let it in. Call out, "Satan, get off me in Jesus' name." Or ask, "Is this love?" Darkness must flee in the presence of love.

The only power fear can have in your life is the power you give it by the confession of your mouth. If we give in to fear, we will not rise to what God has planned for us next, meaning we can never accomplish the task. We have to push forward against every stab of fear and rise above it. This is where you can break through to where you've never been before.

We are to walk by faith, trusting in the victorious outcome that we cannot see. Our perspective should focus on how big God is so our problems look small in comparison. Does the giant you are facing only exist in your head? Perhaps you've made a mountain out of a molehill. From God's perspective, it is always smaller than the tiniest molehill, a dot upon a dot.

In Joshua chapter 1, we read how God told Joshua to be bold and strong and not to be afraid for the Lord was with him. This was a command, and his word is still the same for us today; His power is as real and strong now as it was back then. Jesus promised his disciples, "I will never leave you or forsake you." This promise is for us too. When we are born again and enter God's Kingdom, we enter into His promised land. There will be giants to overcome. It won't be easy or glorious. You must conqueror every fear the enemy brings and you need to walk by faith, trusting in your Saviour. Joshua, the mighty warrior, chose to obey and he clung to those words of encouragement with all his might.

I don't know about you, but there are times that I certainly have to cling to God's word with everything I have within me because the giants I see are screaming out at me and I feel the fear taking hold. It is easy to look at the problem you are faced with and complain or speak negatively. We are used to judging with our eyes, but God does not want us to live that way. He has called us to live by faith, believing His word over any other, even when everything seems impossible. Always give a good report of God's goodness and a good report of your situation and life.

In Joshua 5 and 6 we read about the battle of Jericho. Joshua's greatest battle was not the walls of Jericho, but rather, being obedient to what seemed a crazy idea. Joshua was trained for physical battle, a different type of leader than Moses had been. Joshua had to learn to not rely on his previous experiences or his gift for battle strategy. His greatest battle was to obey what seemed so foolish, even if all of his own men thought he had gone crazy.

He looked at the walls of Jericho and sent the singers first. They marched around the city, singing and praising God before the walls ever fell and before they saw the victory. Their battle was to trust God with all their hearts, as we read in Proverbs 3:5, and not lean on their own understanding. They needed to accept God's leadership, keeping him at the forefront of their mind; when we put God first, He will direct our steps. We must regularly adjust our attitudes when things do not go as expected. Will we stand still and trust God, giving Him praise for what He will do? He can always make a way when there seems to be no way.

Whose word is greater in your life, even when all you see are problems? Whose word has the greater authority? God has no equal; God is on your side. Don't surrender to the thoughts of the enemy. Adam surrendered to Satan when he believed the Devil's word above God's. Stand firm and hold your position. Cling to and love the word of God with all your might and all your heart. It is impossible for God's word to fail because He and His word are one; He is all-powerful and all-knowing.

You can win the battle of putting God's word above your own. Don't fight against God; obey Him and you won't go wrong. We must conquer our hearts and minds before we can overcome outside trials. The first battle is deciding if we will keep a good attitude and have a good response. Will we forgive others? Will we obey God and agree with His word, even when we don't understand His ways? The greatest battle is within ourselves.

Jesus dealt with the spirit of fear once and for all on the cross. There is no fear in God's Kingdom; if God is love and his Kingdom rules in me, that means there is no fear in me. According to 1 John 4:18, "There is no fear in love." When you meditate on how much Jesus loves you, fear will be driven out. When you know God's love for you, when you know He is your Father and will protect you, when you know His favour, and when you know His words are true, there is no fear. Accepting that you are made in His image and that you are safe in His arms, there is no fear. God is love and His perfect love drives out all fear.

I used to be ruled by fear because of my past, but I am not who I was in the past. I have been set free and do not need to base my life on it. You can be free from fear because Jesus has paid the price and conquered all fear, death and disease; he rose to life as an undefeated champion. We can overcome by the blood of the lamb and the word of our testimony, as in Revelation 12:11. Give a great testimony and a good report.

9

GIANT KILLER

In 1 Samuel 16 and 17, we read the story of a young shepherd boy named David. He had fiery red hair and was strong and handsome, though a bit rough around the edges. He spent most of his time alone in the fields, looking after the sheep, which left their smell on him. One day, the prophet Samuel came to Bethlehem to see David's father, Jesse. Samuel invited him and all of his sons to the sacrifice. God had instructed Samuel to anoint one of the children as King over Israel.

Jesse brought out his sons, showing them off to the prophet Samuel with excitement. First, there was Eliab, the eldest, who looked kingly. Samuel thought, "Surely the Lord's anointed stands here before the Lord." But the Lord said to Samuel, "Do not consider his appearance or his height, for I have rejected him. The Lord does not look at the things people look at. People look at the outward appearance, but the Lord looks at the heart."

When God chooses you, people may be confused. You may not look like much, or be as talented or outgoing as some, but love and faithfulness are far more important. God sees your heart and He sees your future. Some people may be gifted, but their character could be lacking humility and a servant's heart.

One after the other, the remaining seven sons of Jesse came to stand before Samuel. The prophet looked intently at them and said, "The Lord has not chosen these. Are these all the sons you have?" Jesse had not brought his youngest son for consideration. "There is still the youngest," Jesse answered. "He is tending the sheep." Samuel said, "Send for him; we will not sit down until he arrives."

David was brought before him and Samuel anointed David as the future king of Israel. The Lord said, "Rise and anoint him; this is the one." Much time would pass before he could be king, but God saw the heart of David—what others could not see.

There came a day when Jesse called David and told him to take some lunch to his brothers who were out on the battlefield. When David arrived, he saw the unimaginable—the entire Israelite army was struck with fear.

The Israelites were on one hill and the Philistines were on the other; in the middle stood a giant over nine feet tall called Goliath. He represented the Philistine army and was waiting to see who would represent the army of Israel to fight him. Goliath shouted to the ranks of Israel, striking terror into their hearts. "Choose a man and have him come down to me. If he is able to fight and kill me, we will become your subjects; but if I overcome him and kill him, you will become our subjects and serve us." Then the Philistine said, "This day I defy the armies of Israel! Give me a man and let us fight each other."

On hearing Goliath's words, Saul and the Israelites did not know what to do. No one dared fight the towering giant, not even King Saul. David had seen similar threatening environments before in the fields and he had dealt with them head-on. This time, there was also a prize to be won. The Israelites said, "Do you see how this man keeps coming out? He comes out to defy Israel. The king will give great wealth to the man who kills him. He will also give him his daughter in marriage and will exempt his family from taxes in Israel."

"I will fight Goliath," David said to Saul. "Let no one lose heart on account of this Philistine; your servant will go and fight him." Though still a youth, David was the only person on the battlefield who was not governed by fear; he rose to the challenge. The fear was not something physical, it was in the heart. David was not afraid because he had already dealt with fear in his life. Fear is fear, whether great or small, but it is a spirit that you can overcome.

David spent many years in the fields looking after the sheep; he had fought a bear and a lion to protect them. David said to Saul, "Your servant has been keeping his father's sheep. When a lion or a bear came and carried off a sheep from the flock, I went after it, struck it and rescued the sheep from its mouth. When it turned on me, I seized it by its hair, struck it and killed it. Your servant has killed both the lion and the bear; this uncircumcised Philistine will be like one of them, because he has defied the armies of the living God."

David saw Goliath was like the bear who was the same height when standing on his hind legs, and he saw the Israelite army as sheep. David knew that God had protected him and rescued him from every threat he had ever faced, and because of this he had full confidence in the Lord. He confidently expected to defeat Goliath because he was not looking at the size of the giant before him; he was looking at the faithfulness of God.

During his time looking after the sheep, David played the harp and spent a lot of time singing and worshiping God, thanking him and asking for help in difficult situations. He got to know God personally and discovered his faithfulness. David had killed the lion and the bear that were much stronger than him; he knew God had the power to help him. It was nothing in his own doing or his own strength; he humbly relied upon God. David knew God was for him and would give him the victory. If you're worried about an outcome, fill your mind with God's track record. Think about how he has been there for you in the past. Has he ever truly let you down?

When you are faced with giants, remember how you overcame the last one and how God was with you. This one may look fiercer, but God is as powerful as he always has been and you are stronger than you were in the past. David did not think, "What if I fail, I will look a right fool." Rather, he thought, "I cannot let this giant win, I cannot let the Israelites be slaves to these Philistines." When David defeated Goliath, everyone cheered with him because they all had won and were free from the evil one. When Jesus died on the cross, we were all set free. There is something worth fighting for and it is much bigger than you or me. When you overcome your giants you become a stronger and better person; your life is improved and as a result, you can help change the lives of others.

Saul saw David as an inexperienced young man whom he surely believed would be killed by the giant. He offered David his own armour but David could not wear it. "I cannot go in these," he said to Saul, "because I am not used to them." He took them off and went as himself, trusting God and doing what he knew best in his own way. You can do the same and defeat your giants with the skills God has given you. Be you!

Goliath laughed and mocked David as he approached. "Then he took his staff in his hand, chose five smooth stones from the stream, put them in the pouch of his shepherd's bag and, with his sling in his hand, approached the Philistine. David said to the Philistine, 'You come against me with sword and spear and javelin, but I come against you in the name of the Lord Almighty, the God of the armies of Israel, whom you have defied. This day the Lord will deliver you into my hands, and I'll strike you down and cut off your head. All those gathered here will know that it is not by sword or spear that the Lord saves; for the battle is the Lord's and he will give all of you into our hands.'"

David gave a good report of what would happen by declaring his trust in God. Then he did exactly as he'd said—he came at Goliath as if he were a bear and killed him. David was a champion giant killer; he killed the giant of fear and intimidation within his heart long ago.

God had a plan to promote David; he had been anointed as the future king and this event revealed his strength and courage to the public. He was being prepared for kingship. It is through your tough times and your private struggles that you grow.

God brought David from the solitary fields, where no one saw him or knew him, into the public eye. If he had stayed in the fields, he would never have experienced his greatest life-changing challenge of defeating Goliath the giant. He would never have become King. We must not be afraid of new territory and new giants; they will propel us forward into what God has prepared next.

David learnt to trust God to protect and guide him when harm came near the sheep. Killing the lion and the bear was David's training to become king, ready to rule and ready to conquer. He had to be faithful in the unseen place of his heart before he could be faithful in the public eye.

David faced his giants when no one was looking, no one cared, and no one cheered. Now he faced the giants in public for all to see and he was certain of God's protection. He knew God's love and favour; he knew God's grace and strength. David believed in who God was and what He could do. David's character had been refined, and he grabbed hold of the opportunity to be a giant killer. He faced his fears and overcame them, becoming a victorious champion.

10

THE PROMISED LAND

When we think of the "promised land," we tend to think of one day arriving in Heaven; we think of eternal life, no more suffering or pain. The Bible tells us about Heaven and God's eternal Kingdom. Heaven is a real place where we will one day meet God face to face and dwell with him. It is our promised land where there is no more pain or suffering. At John 14:1-3, Jesus tells us not to worry because he has gone to prepare a place for us.

Suppose we think of entering the "promised land" as when we become born again into God's Kingdom, the land of abundance and eternal life? We can enjoy all of God's goodness and his Kingdom now. We can experience all that Jesus accomplished for us on the cross. But this can't possibly be the "promised land" because there are problems to solve, difficulties to overcome, and giants roam the land. This can't be God's best; surely, we left the wilderness for good?

The bible tells us in John 16:33 that in this life on Earth, we will experience trials. "I have told you these things, so that in me you may have peace. In this world you will have trouble. But take heart! I have overcome the world." We have not arrived home; we are in a foreign land where the rules of the kingdom are different. Instead of love your enemy, it's killing him; instead of loyalty, it's doing what is best for you; and instead of a land where there is no sickness, this place has been full of it ever since Adam and Eve gave their authority on the Earth to Satan by believing and obeying his word over God's word.

We live in a fallen world, but within us, we have the peace of God that is beyond human understanding. We have the power of the Holy Spirit and can experience indescribable joy, even when problems surround us. We develop an unshakeable trust in God and His Word, and so bring back His authority on the Earth that He originally intended for us.

We pray, "Your kingdom come, your will be done on this earth as it is in Heaven." God's will is done on the Earth through our obedience and partnering with Him; the Holy Spirit lives in us and with us and teaches us all things. His power is at work within us to bring about God's will, to lay hands on the sick that they will recover, to set the captives free, and to preach the good news of the gospel of God's kingdom. By the power of the Holy Spirit, blind eyes open to the truth and receive the gifts God has given us of eternal and abundant life.

Jesus has commanded us not to be afraid, but to take possession of what he has already given us, though there may be giants in the land, problems to solve, or opposition to face. We are commanded to be strong and to take rulership and dominion; this is exactly what God commanded the Israelites to do when they entered the Promised Land. See Joshua chapter 1.

What were God's people told there would be in the Promised Land? It was God's gift to His people; it was a spacious land flowing with milk and honey, lush green grass and fresh grapes. The Promised Land was a place where they could settle, be free from slavery, live a good life, and multiply. They would have all their needs met and be healthy with good nourishment from the land. It was a place they could call home, where God would be their God and they would be his people, living within his Kingdom rules and principles for a blessed, prosperous, and flourishing life. Rich and bountiful, a land of plenty.

It was a place where they could be victorious and have the courage to rise up and take a stand. But the land wasn't without giants and the people who already lived there were not going to just release their territory; they stubbornly refused and fought to keep it. God did not promise life would be easy, but they may have expected the Promised Land to be like an all-inclusive holiday. No such luck! There were going to be many battles to fight in order to possess the land.

God promised that He was with them and had already given them the land. They were not to be afraid, but be bold, strong, and courageous, as it was certain they would be victorious. God always keeps His promises. Challenges help us grow and mature; there is no such life as one without challenges, and there will always be giants in the land. If there were no difficulties, we would be weak, lazy, and immature. Our physical muscles grow when under pressure, and our spiritual muscles and character develop the same way.

What are we promised today? God promises that He will never leave us or forsake us. We are also guaranteed in His word that if we obey His teachings within His Kingdom rule, then we will reap the benefits of our choice. We will be blessed and not cursed, we will live long, healthy lives, and all will go well for us, as noted in Deuteronomy 30. God has laid it all out before us and gives us the choice to follow Him. He loves us and desires that we will choose wisely.

We may have been promised many things by many people, but when we finally got what we wanted, it wasn't at all how we imagined. Could this really be the Promised Land? "Surely not! This couldn't be it; there are giants and challenges here in the land. Is this really what God promised me? It's not at all how I imagined; I was hoping for a happier life. This can't be the life God has designed for me. I thought He liked me, so why all this trouble?"

At last, when you thought everything was going well, some difficulty arose to spoil the fun and halt your progress. The enemy is standing at the gate; he will always oppose you and does not want you to take possession of new ground. He does not want you to enter into God's Kingdom, or to realize all that God has made possible for you now because of Jesus' sacrifice on the cross. He will try to block you from getting to the next victory. When we are surrounded by problems and giants and the enemy is at the gate, what are we to do? The bible says in James 4:7, "Submit yourselves, then, to God, Resist the devil, and he will flee from you."

The devil detests our worship to God and hates the presence of Him. When we are blocked from moving forward, we fight not flesh and blood. We bow down and worship God, or we sing His praises and lift Jesus high; we declare His goodness and we walk in love and faith. The Devil will flee and the gate will open for you to move forward again.

11

VICTORIOUS LIVING

To live a victorious life, you need a victor's mentality. You are what you think and you will do what you think about, but you can never be greater than your thoughts. "Whether you think you can, or you think you can't – you're right," Henry Ford.

We have all fallen victim at some point in our lives. We can choose to stay a victim, afraid of moving forward and of what lies ahead, afraid of failure or of success. We can be afraid of what people think or of getting hurt again. We can stick with what we are used to because it is easier, staying in our comfort zones and attempting to be in complete control of our lives. Or, we can be a victor, conquering every fear and jumping into the unknown. We can live an overcoming and victorious life.

Romans 8:31-32 says, "What, then, shall we say in response to these things? If God is for us, who can be against us? He who did not spare his own Son, but gave him up for us all— how will he not also, along with him, graciously give us all things?" And verse 37-38 says, "No, in all these things we are more than conquerors through him who loved us. For I am convinced that neither death nor life, neither angels nor demons, neither the present nor the future, nor any powers, neither height nor depth, nor anything else in all creation, will be able to separate us from the love of God that is in Christ Jesus our Lord."

The best life we can have is the result of having a victorious mindset; we need to set our minds to win, knowing that God is for us one hundred per cent. If God gave His only son to die for us, why would He withhold love or success? We must trust God's love for us and settle, fasten, and lock our thoughts on what is good. We are to be like an athlete who is a runner. He does not run out onto the track wondering whether he will win or not and he doesn't say to the others, "I don't think I will win today." He has no room for doubt.

The racer runs for one purpose only, and that is to win. He has chosen the attitude of a victor. He trusts in himself, he has trained well, and he believes he will win. We need to train our minds by renewing them with the truths in God's Word, believing who he says we are and what he says we can do. The more you read the verses in the bible, the more you will begin to believe they're for you. Then run each day's race like a champion. We must believe and speak as a victor in order to be a victor.

We are to continually speak God's Word throughout our lives for our health, thoughts and future. Your heart believes what you plant in it; sow good thoughts and good words. Carrot seeds are sown, planted in soil, and are regularly watered and fed. A full-grown carrot is the result. As you sow and water, the seed will grow into faith within the soil of your heart.

God has a great plan for us but if we constantly say, "Oh, no, he doesn't," then God's hands are tied because we are going against Him and His Word. We tend to battle with His Word when we should be surrendering, knowing that He knows best. Many Christians face this internal battle of the heart; will we agree with Him or follow our own way of thinking?

The way you talk to yourself is very important, so hold on to God's Word with all your heart. We see an example of this in Matthew 9 with a woman who had been subject to bleeding for twelve years. She could have given up on her hope of ever becoming well again. She could have seen every doctor in the country and spent every penny she had. But instead of giving up and feeling like a victim of her lot in life, she talked to herself in Verse 21 and said, "If only I can touch the hem of his garment I will be healed." What great expectation that showed—a mindset and attitude of a victor, a true champion. She did not settle for defeat; she did exactly what she set out to do and was healed by Jesus.

I come into contact with many people at work every day. One particular day, I spoke to a lady who had a problem with her eyesight which was getting worse. I prayed with her for miraculous healing but then she spoke from her heart telling me she had lost all hope. She said, "Thank you, but I think I need to accept the fact." Her feelings of hopelessness were bigger than her faith to ask me for prayer. I explained that as she focused on God's love for her and thanked Him daily for giving her wonderful sight, her heart and faith would get stronger. When you believe, your whole body becomes full of light.

Who are we to say God can't fix us or solve our problems? Who are we to say, "Poor me, I will just have to put up with it because we are living in a fallen world?" This is not what our creator teaches.

Years ago, I had a motorbike accident that damaged my cruciate ligament. I had an operation but one night as I lay in bed my leg felt like it was stretching out towards the footboard uncontrollably. I felt like Reed Richards, "Mr Fantastic" from the film "Fantastic Four." My leg did not stop stretching until the artificial carbon fibre ligament snapped with a sharp sting. Although I exercised, for over a year my knee joint was prone to collapse and I would fall to the floor, unable to walk on it for days. Many people had prayed for me as I feared I would never dance again. This was difficult for me as I loved to dance in praise. I had been a dancer and prima ballerina for years. As I woke up one morning, I spoke to the Lord in my heart. I said, "Lord, I know you love me and I am safe in your hands. I am going to take the chance and dance without fear of falling. I am in your hands. You created me, I will dance for you and you care for me. I pray you will keep me strong." And every time I danced, I said in my heart, "Lord, this is up to you, I am in your hands."

I had received a miracle—from that day on, my knee has not collapsed. More recently, I was walking through town and I slowed down because my knee became painful and did not want to bear my weight. This was hindering my life and progress, so I thought like a victim. As I walked, I quoted scriptures about healing as I had been doing for a while. "Heal me, o Lord, and I will be healed; thank you, Lord, that by your stripes I am healed." But deep down, I was fed up with my situation. Instead of focusing on what could be, I only focused on the pain I felt. I asked the Lord, "Why isn't quoting scripture working for me? And why after years of being healed, is it now plaguing me? Show me, Lord, how to receive."

I felt I should concentrate on relaxing every part of my body, walking slowly, and breathing deeply. As I did this, I found myself confessing, "Thank you, Lord, I am in the best shape of my life." A connection occurred, like two electrical wires meeting and giving off a spark. This confession came from my heart with a smile that ran through my whole being. I felt the joy and I believed the words I spoke. So I sang a little song under my breath, "I am in the best shape of my life, thank you, Lord; by your stripes, I am healed." I sang it over and over because it lit me up inside with joy, belief, and praise.

My bold confession was based on God's word and His will for my life. I discovered that speaking God's word over my life was not enough—I needed to believe it in my heart. We need to constantly speak God's word over our lives until it takes root in our hearts. Romans 10:9 says, "If you declare **with**

your mouth, "Jesus is Lord," and **believe in your heart** that God raised him from the dead, you will be saved." Confession alone is not enough. We are to confess with our mouth and believe in our heart. Speak words that you believe and can connect with. Your smile and good thoughts run through your body and you become full of light and life. Jesus is life and gives life and light to our whole beings. His word is alive, powerful, and active—Hebrews 4:12.

Imagine that you can be exactly what you predict, creating your day and your life with what you speak. This is an actual possibility because you are made in God's image and in Genesis 1:3 he said, "Let there be light," and it was so. What was visible was made out of what was not visible when He spoke it into being. So, we must be careful with our words.

When words are released into the atmosphere, they become substance. If you want a better, victorious, wonderful life, it starts with your mouth. Your brain makes sure your body obeys and lines up with the words you speak out of your mouth and believe in your heart.

Believing is the key; you can tell if someone believes he is a winner by his mouth and his attitude. If he is discouraged his light will go out, his shoulders will slump, the corners of his mouth will turn down, and he will lose all joy. But if he thinks about his trip to the Bahamas the following week, he would immediately smile and be full of light, forgetting what was troubling him. We can choose to change our focus and what we dwell on. Philippians 4:8 reads, "Finally, brothers and sisters, whatever is true, whatever is noble, whatever is right, whatever is pure, whatever is lovely, whatever is admirable—if anything is excellent or praiseworthy—think about such things."

In Judges Chapter 6, there was a man named Gideon. God surprised him one day when He called him a "mighty man of valour." Gideon asked, "Who, me?" He didn't feel mighty, he didn't act mighty, and he didn't believe he was mighty. But

God sees who we can be if we put our trust in Him. Gideon adapted to his true identity, the way God saw him at his full potential. With his new mindset, he was finally free to be himself, a champion. Just like we can reset our bodies with healthy food, we can reset our minds with spiritual food. We need a plate of God's word every day.

Choose to be a victor by remembering that God has the final authority in your life. Stand up for truth and speak the truth. Have the obedient attitude of someone who never considers himself as a victim but declares, "I am more than a conqueror."

The bible says we have the ability to renew our minds and choose our attitudes by walking in God's love with the Holy Spirit living within us. Jesus defeated Satan at the cross for us and rose victoriously.

Every day we face the battle within our hearts about whether or not we will follow God's way. How will we respond to the person being rude to us? Will we give that lady a gospel tract? Will we pray for that man or talk ourselves out of it because we're unsure if he will reject our kindness? My pastor recently preached a message where he said, "You cannot serve two masters at the same time." He added, "You can't obey two thoughts at the same time, so which one are you going to follow?"

Which thought will you allow to be your master? God has given you everything you need; he has equipped you to live a victorious life, but you must do your part and believe God's thoughts about you over everyone else's, including your own. God knows every problem you face and has equipped you for it already.

You can declare with your mouth and believe in your heart, "I AM living a victorious life. I am a victor and I am a champion overcomer."

When it seems everything is going wrong and everyone is against you, or when you are feeling the pressure from every side, head in your hands, wondering where to go from here and what to do next, think about Paul and Silas in prison. They were put in jail for disrupting the peace and doing what they thought was right. We read in Acts.16:16-34 that Paul and Silas were on their way to the place of prayer. On the way, they cast a fortune-telling spirit out of a slave girl. The owners of the slave girl realised their money-maker had been exorcised and seized Paul and Silas. The slave owners had the men stripped and flogged before they were thrown into prison. They sat in silence in the dark gloomy cell, bruised and in great pain; this is not what they had signed up for. Should they call it a day and give it all up as a bad job?

Paul and Silas had no human strength left within them, yet they did not grumble or complain. Instead, they sat there pondering their circumstances and remembering who was ultimately in control of their lives. They finally spoke to one another and shot up arrow prayers of thanks. They magnified the Lord with their mouths and their hearts, and before they knew it, they were mouthing the words of a song. As they pushed through the pain, the words slipped from their tongues like oil, and they sang wonderful praise with everything they had within them. If I were there with Paul in place of Silas that day, I may have said, "A fine mess you've got us into, Paul. This is your fault. If you hadn't opened your big mouth we wouldn't be in this dire situation."

What happened next was a miracle. A violent earthquake shook the building and the doors of the prison flew open. The chains of all the prisoners fell off and they were free. The same can be said today—when you praise God, your chains fall off! You are set free from whatever held you captive. When you glorify God in all circumstances, he shows up in great power for you and for all onlookers that may believe and be saved.

The jailer and his family were saved and baptised. But it can be a fight when the last thing you feel like doing is praising God. Every bit of your body resists, nothing wants to open your mouth and speak positive thoughts out loud or glorify God. Praise is an awesome weapon, making the walls come down. When we lift God up, He lifts us up. To live a victorious life we need to be singing victory songs of praise.

When we are faced with difficult circumstances and all seems lost, we have a choice of how to respond. Don't give up or get discouraged, just look to Jesus and sing his praise. When we respond with joy and praise, we are training our minds to focus on how big God is, magnifying Him and not the problem. Thank Him because your victory is on its way. We can persevere and be steadfast with our faith in God, knowing that He is with us and wants to strengthen us. When we praise God and trust in Him, He can work on our behalf. But when we worry, God has nothing to work with. Faith is the chariot that God can ride upon.

Whatever you are facing today, you can overcome; even if you're sick and medicine has failed you, if your finances are out of control, if your family seems to be falling apart, or if bad habits have you hopelessly bound. If you've done absolutely all you know to do and you still haven't gotten results, then let go and let God take control. When we try to fix problems ourselves, God will let us try, but when we surrender to Him and thank Him, He can work in us and through us and He will give us the keys to success.

I have discovered that in my own strength I can endlessly struggle, but then I lay it down and say, "God, please help me, I can't do this anymore. I am overwhelmed and I keep failing over and over again. I give up striving in my own strength and totally surrender to you." That is when God steps in to help me. I have found that the key is to offer complete surrender and let Jesus be Lord in every area of my life. My greatest battle has been letting go of what I thought I could control. I have had to stop playing the "blame game" and instead, take responsibility for my attitude. The greatest battle was in my heart, not in what I could see around me.

If you are struggling in any area, then it may be that you haven't fully surrendered. Everything belongs to the Lord, including you. If you have accepted Jesus Christ as your Lord and Saviour then you are no longer your own; you belong to God. You were bought with the price of Jesus' precious blood. He gave his all for you and held nothing back.

Today is a good day to surrender to God. Give Him your all and see what He will do. He loves you immensely and wants to both help and bless you. Jesus is your answer, whether you need a friend, spouse, Father, helper, comforter, or even a protector—he is your all. Stick close and live a blessed victorious life, full of joy and strength.

12

THE WORD BECAME FLESH

We have heard it said, "You are what you eat." We need to eat food daily to stay healthy and alive; the food we eat becomes part of us. If I eat too many of the wrong foods, such as cake and ice cream, or too many carbohydrates, my body knows it. The next day I struggle to think clearly and I become sluggish.

We are affected by what we physically eat. Likewise, we are affected by what we let into our gateways—our ears and eyes. When we read the word of God and truly take it in by thinking about it and chewing it over, we are digesting it. We eat of God's word and it takes effect in our thinking, our hearts and our lives; it changes our levels of joy and challenges wrong thinking. His word shows us where we are going wrong and helps us to repent and change our ways. It causes us to treat people better and strengthens us to boldly deal with problems. The word of God can enrich and truly transform our lives. Hebrews 4:12 says, "For the word of God is alive and active. Sharper than any double-edged sword, it penetrates even to dividing soul and spirit, joints and marrow; it judges the thoughts and attitudes of the heart."

In John 1:1-5 we read, "In the beginning was the **Word**, and the Word was with God, and the Word was God. **He** was with God in the beginning. Through **him** all things were made; without **him** nothing was made that has been made. In **him** was life, and that life was the light of all mankind. The light shines in the darkness, and the darkness has not overcome it." We could say, "In the beginning was Jesus, Jesus was with God and was God."

John 1:14 shows, "The Word became flesh and made his dwelling among us." Jesus is the word that gives life—we eat of him, we eat his words, we obey them, we live according to them, and we become the word in action. The word becomes flesh through our lives too. His word in me becomes flesh, the truth in action. His word feeds me and I become the word.

Jesus says in John 15:1, "I am the true vine, and my Father is the gardener." You are an extension of Jesus—you are a branch that extends from the true vine. The same sap that runs through the vine also runs through its connected branches. You could say the same blood, same creativity and same life, are running through you. You are connected to, belonging to, attached to, and the same as; you feed on his very life, one with him. In verse 5 Jesus says, "I am the vine; you are the branches. If you remain in me and I in you, you will bear much fruit; apart from me you can do nothing."

In John 15:9-14 we read, "As the father has loved me, so I have loved you. Now remain in my love. If you obey my commands you will remain in my love just as I have obeyed my father's commands and remain in his love. I have told you this so that my joy may be in you and that your joy may be complete. My command is this; love each other as I have loved you. Greater love has no one than this that he lay down his life for his friends you are my friends if you do what I command."

Verse16 says, "You did not choose me but I chose you and appointed you to go and bear fruit through that will last then the father will give you whatever you ask in my name this is my command love each other."

We read in verse 11, "I have told you this so that my joy may be in you and that your joy may be complete." But how may our joy be complete? He has told us the answer, so let's go to the verse above to find out what it is he has told us. He says in verse 9, "As the father has loved me so I have loved you, now remain in my love. If you obey my commands you will remain in my love." That is how we remain in his love, by obeying his commands. "Just as I have obeyed my father's commands and remain in his love. I have told you this so that my joy may be in you and that your joy may be complete."

The key to having complete joy is to obey his commands. Since we love him, we do not want to stray from his commands because that is not the nature of love. In verse 11 He says, "I have told you this so that **my joy** may be in you and that your joy may be complete." Our joy is not complete unless we have the joy of Jesus. We must obey his commands, which is where we find Jesus' joy, as well as our own.

Jesus did not operate on this Earth on his own command alone; he only did what he saw his Father doing. In John 14:8-10 we read, "Philip said, "Lord, show us the Father and that will be enough for us." Jesus answered: "Don't you know me, Philip, even after I have been among you such a long time? Anyone who has seen me has seen the Father. How can you say, 'Show us the Father'? Don't you believe that I am in the Father, and that the Father is in me? The words I say to you I do not speak on my own authority. Rather, it is the Father, living in me, who is doing his work."

Jesus and the Father are one. Jesus desires that we are one with him just as he is one with the Father. We have been born again with the very life of God within us. Just like the vine and branches have the same sap running through, we have His nature of love and "love" himself lives within us. We have been rescued from the Kingdom of darkness and belong to the Kingdom of light and love. We are an extension of God and

His Kingdom and we can continue to extend His Kingdom, by continually being an extension of God and His love.

When we have love, peace and kindness within us, it is displayed by our outward physical bodies. If you have inner turmoil and confusion, then it is shown by your outward physical body and behaviour. Who we are on the inside extends both to the outside and to other people. We are each defined as a person by our inward life, where we communicate with God and where we think and believe. The way we continually think is the way we become. We are disciples, learning to hold onto all that Jesus taught and his word sets us free. John 8:31-32 reads, "To the Jews who had believed him, Jesus said, "If you hold to my teaching, you are really my disciples. Then you will know the truth, and the truth will set you free."

Every provision we need for life is found in Jesus. I love what Derek Prince says in his book, "The Divine Exchange." He states, "Believing and thanking, thanking and believing, are like a spiral staircase that will take you continually higher into the fullness of God's provision." To me, this means the more we thank Him, the more we believe and therefore receive. In turn, the more we believe, the more we want to thank Him. This brings about a close connection and the freedom to access and receive all that God has for us. This is an awesome cycle. We stay connected to the vine, we eat of Him—of His life-giving words—and the word becomes flesh. The word becomes alive and active in our life; Jesus is the word and he lives in me, his word feeds me and I become the word.

13

TWO KINGDOMS

Every single person on the planet, including you and me, belong to a kingdom. There are many countries, nations, and governments on this Earth, but there are only two spiritual kingdoms. There is the Kingdom of light and love, which is the Kingdom of God, and there is the Kingdom of darkness, which is the Kingdom of Satan.

When we were born, we did not have a choice into which Kingdom we belonged. We were born into a kingdom full of envy, pride and ego where there is darkness, depression and decay. But in God's Kingdom the opposite is true—love rules, so there is joy, peace, patience, goodness, kindness, and self-control. In Matthew 6:10, Jesus taught his disciples to pray, "Your kingdom come, your will be done on earth as it is in heaven." This means God's Kingdom, as it is in Heaven, can be experienced on the Earth even today.

In the Kingdom of God, there is no sickness and no disease, there is no poverty, no depression, and no defeat! We can experience healing, wholeness, joy, prosperity and victory. Jesus left his home in Heaven to show us the way of his father, to show us how the Kingdom of love and of light operates—how God operates. This also shows us that when we are born again into His Kingdom, we are under new kingdom rules.

As God's children, we take on a new nature and become like Him. We do things differently; our desires change and the world no longer revolves around ourselves. If we fall back into our old nature of envy, strife, or unkindness, we should turn around, repent and jump back into where we belong without delay, to operate in the Kingdom of love.

Jesus came to Earth to rescue us from the Kingdom of darkness under Satan's rule. In Colossians 1:13 we read, "For He has rescued us from darkness and brought us into the kingdom of the son he loves." No one can see or enter the kingdom of God unless he is born again. John 3:3 says, "Jesus replied, "Very truly I tell you, no one can see the kingdom of God unless they are born again." When you become born again, you are given a new heart. It is no longer a heart of stone, but a heart of flesh. This new spirit is found in the book of Ezekiel: 36:26, "I will give you a new heart and put a new spirit in you; I will remove from you your heart of stone and give you a heart of flesh."

In the beginning, God created man and woman to have fellowship and communion with Him as His children. We can read the story of the fall of mankind in Genesis chapter 3 when Eve was tempted by Satan. Adam and Eve ate from the tree and fell into temptation, obeying Satan's word over God's word, and everything changed—not just for them, but for the entire human bloodline. For the first time, Adam and Eve experienced pain, depression, suffering, jealousy, anxiety and all things belonging to the Kingdom of darkness.

We have all been born into this same kingdom ever since. If you have any doubts, look at the Ten Commandments. You will see we fall short of the standards of our awesome creator God; no sin can appear in His Holy presence. But God had a plan to help His children. He was the first to sacrifice an animal and shed its blood. While the skin was still warm and wet with blood, He covered Adam and Eve with it as a sin covering so that He could look upon them and communicate with them.

God taught the people how to sacrifice a lamb every year to cover the sins of the people, but that's all it could do—the blood of an animal could never completely cleanse us, only cover us over. You will find this in the book of Hebrews, chapter 10. Jesus died on the cross as the perfect lamb, the perfect sacrifice. He shed his precious blood for all the people on the Earth, past, present, and future. We who accept his sacrifice are now justified by the blood of Jesus, as though we had never sinned, according to Romans 5:1. The blood of Jesus does not cover over our sins like the blood of an animal, but rather completely washes it away. Psalm 103:12 says, "As far as the east is from the west, so far has he removed our transgressions from us."

When Jesus died on the cross, the land went dark. Jesus cried out, "My God, My God, why have you forsaken me?" in Mark 15:34. The intimacy he had with the Father was broken; God could not look at the sin that Jesus took upon himself. Jesus died for our sins and accepted the punishment we deserved. In this divine exchange, Jesus was separated from the Father in our place, so that we can be reconciled to Him. We can have intimacy with our heavenly father and boldly come before His throne, as it says in Hebrews 4:16. What awesome love! Jesus took our badness away and gave us his goodness in its place.

It is important to know which Kingdom you belong to— the light or the dark. It is also critical to realise that this is your choice. Jesus has already paid the price for you by dying on the cross for your sins, he has made the way. All who will believe in him, accept his sacrifice, and call upon him shall be saved as stated in Romans 10:13. We shall give glory to God forever and live in His Kingdom, with His power and authority.

The option to access Heaven is ours; Jesus showed his great love for us. He desires us to be with him now and forever, but it is up to us to decide. Do we accept his offer for a gift of life within his family, as was God's original plan? In Luke 15, we read the parable of the lost son who wanted his inheritance early—off he went into the world and made a big mess; he lost everything, but eventually came to his senses. When he returned home, his father saw him in the distance and ran out to meet him with open arms. Our Heavenly Father waits for us with open arms.

If you are ever unsure, extend thanks to God anyway. The more we thank God, the more we believe in what He has done for us. Do you know to which Kingdom you belong? Don't wait to decide because it is the most important decision you will ever make. It is an eternal decision that will not only affect your today but your tomorrow and all of your future.

Without Jesus in your life, there is no real lasting change that can take place. You can change your life in your own strength and have a small measure of success, but you will always struggle. You will end up back at rock bottom because you don't have the power of God in your life. We can say all the right things and do good deeds, but without the power of Jesus in our lives, the results cannot last. Every answer to every problem you could ever need is in Jesus; if you have Jesus, you have everything.

You can pray today, asking Jesus to forgive all of your sins—it doesn't matter who you are, where you come from, or what you have done.

Let's pray…

Dear heavenly Father, please forgive me of all my sins. I'm truly sorry. Jesus, come into my heart today and save my soul. I believe you lived, you died and you rose again from the dead. Jesus, be the Lord of my life now and forevermore and write my name in Heaven's book of life. In Jesus name, Amen.

14

I AM - THE 31 DAY CHALLENGE

The power of what we think, say and believe shapes our lives. We are creative beings because God has designed us in His image. This chapter has 31 affirmations for you to speak over your life—one for every day of the month. I have included scriptures for some of the days as a reference.

You can come against every negative thought holding you back from becoming all you can be and begin taking steps toward your goals. We believe what we say about ourselves more than what anyone else says; it is important to speak out loud into the atmosphere so our own ears can hear it, God can hear it, the Devil can hear it, and the atmosphere around you can hear it. My pastor preached a moving message called, "The Problem Has Ears." You can speak to the problem. Your ears are affected by what they hear; what you confess and believe changes your life. You become your thoughts in action and your life reflects the decisions you make every day.

What you choose to wear today, whether you are grumpy or happy, and whether you reach your goals or not, all depends on your thoughts and the decisions you make. Change your speech and expectation of what you believe and you will change your life.

When you make affirmations, also called confessions, or repeat other phrases, you are affirming it to yourself. You are making it a solid ground for your belief system to stand upon. Base your confessions on Jesus and his word; he is the solid rock on which we stand and all other ground is sinking sand. Affirmations will impact you whether you speak positively or negatively, so you may as well agree with what the God of the universe says.

Like taking medicine, declare God's goodness in your life out loud and say something good about yourself, your day, and your life three times each day.

DAY 1

This is the day the Lord has made. I will rejoice in it and be glad in it. I am full of thankfulness and praise, thanking Jesus for all he has done. He has enriched my entire life and given me a greater understanding of the truth. I am expecting great things to happen today because the Great I Am is with me—Psalm 118:24.

DAY 2

My journey may have been long, sometimes rough and sometimes smooth, but I have arrived at today. I am celebrating God's goodness and guidance, and how far He has brought me. With Him, I look to the future and dream big. Today is the day to live life on purpose and live life to the full. All of Heaven is cheering me on.

DAY 3

I will keep singing and rejoicing with great expectation. God wants me to ask Big because whatever I ask is small to him. He can do immeasurably more than I can ask, think or imagine. I ask Big, think Big and dream Big.

Jesus came to give me not just life, but life in all its fullness. I am living life large and to the full. I have the life of God in me; I have his love, his nature and his ability.

DAY 4

I am excited about God today and what He will do, both in me and through me. I am expecting great things and I have a great attitude. I am a cheerful champion ready to overcome any obstacle and I have the ability to make great decisions. I am in Christ, have the mind of Christ, and I am looking forward to a great day.

I am healthy, cheerful and optimistic. I have great opportunities for the Gospel; I am designed for greatness. I am sharing the love of Jesus wherever I am—I make a difference.

DAY 5

I love my Bible—it is the word of God. It is life and health to my bones and I read it every day. I am who God says I am; I can do whatever He says I can and I have whatever He says I can have. I am thinking more clearly, speaking more positively, and believing the bigger and better.

DAY 6

God's wisdom is available to me; it is my constant companion and never holds anything back from me. Wisdom cries aloud, "Go this way. Don't do that, do this," or "Change direction" and "Think this thought instead of that one."

When I show complete commitment in my ways to the Lord and have total trust in Him, He will guide me by His thoughts, by His Holy Spirit, and by His peace that is greater than all understanding. I will listen to His instruction and I shall dwell in safety. I shall feel at ease and be free from fear of evil or harm. I choose God and His ways, so I have a tremendous advantage in life—Proverbs 1:33

DAY 7

God's role is to carefully shape me, and my role is to remain pliable to allow Him to do amazing things. He is the potter and I am the clay.

When I am pliable, only a small amount of pressure is needed to shape me. But if I, being the clay, am stiff and resistant, more pressure is needed to mould me the way the potter desires. It is best I remain pliable, like putty in His loving hands—Isaiah 64:8

DAY 8

No matter what the day throws at me—anxiety, worry, fear—I can choose how to respond. I can live in defeat or live in the victory God promises me. Today I choose to walk in victory, trusting in Jesus who defeated all, including death.

I am declaring into the atmosphere today that I am a winner. No weapon formed against me shall prosper, says Isaiah 54:17. God is for me, with me, and in me to do great and marvellous things. I am called, chosen and destined; I am a life-changing inspiration.

DAY 9

The plans the Lord has for me are for good and not evil—plans to give me hope and a future. They lead me to prosperity and not to harm. My hope is in the Lord and he places good desires in my heart that come to pass. He gives me life and light. I may make many plans in life, but if I constantly bring them before the Lord, his purpose and plans will prevail. He has a great plan for my life and will direct me—Jeremiah 29:11

DAY 10

An anxious heart weighs a man down. He walks about stooped over and the corners of his mouth drop. But a kind, encouraging word cheers him up and makes his heart glad. Today, I choose to speak happy, loving, cheerful, encouraging words. Today, I drop seeds of kindness as I walk along life's path; I make great confessions over myself and others.

I can tell my direction in life by listening to the words I speak; my words direct the course of my life. I align my words with God's word and His plan.

I deliberately declare the goodness of God and His promises over my life regularly. I am speaking more about the things that are not yet visible, bringing them into reality. "I believe and confess, and so I am."

DAY 11

I speak into the atmosphere; I speak to things that are not yet, as though they are. I speak life into what appears dead and I speak success when I only see failure. I speak joy and peace when I am disturbed; I speak courage when fearful and confidence when timid. I speak love and forgiveness when I feel hurt. God has given me the power of life and death in my tongue, says Proverbs 18:21.

If I can change a thought, then I can change an emotion because they follow my thoughts; my words and actions will follow as well. My emotions do not rule. My spirit rules and I am filled with the Holy Spirit.

I am speaking faith-filled words straight from Heaven. I'm clinging to God's word with all my might; Jesus is life, hope and sure victory in a dark world. I am going to let his light shine.

DAY 12

If I hear the word, read it, and understand it, the word will be multiplied in my life. I will eat of Him who is the word and I will become the word in action. The word, Jesus, lives in me to accomplish his great plan—I am the living, walking, acting word. I become the word; I am the life and representative of Jesus on the Earth.

God's word is my medicine; it keeps me thinking straight. I keep God's word before my eyes and in my ears so it enters my heart. This way I will stay healed and whole and make the right decisions. God's word is life to me and wisdom is the most important thing. Out of my heart flows what is in it—Proverbs 4:20-23.

DAY 13

God's word is a lamp to light my path, showing me the right way to go. I do my work well and He prospers me. I walk in His light, His word, His blessings, and His discipline. I have a disciplined, encouraging mouth. When I walk, God's word and wisdom lead me, when I sleep, His word watches over me, and when I am awake it speaks to me—Proverbs 6:20-22.

I deposit God's words in the bank of my heart, as treasure within, to withdraw them upon my lips and act them out in faith. I store up God's commandments within me and they give me life—Proverbs 7:1.

DAY 14

I am wise—I build my house and prepare in advance. I feed on wisdom and take in her instruction; I drink of her and love her. I am teachable and heed correction. I line up my ways with God's ways rather than take offense at His rebuke. My days shall be multiplied and the years of my life increased and made joyous. Wisdom is my reward—Proverbs 9.

DAY 15

A man is satisfied by the fruit of his mouth. I read the word, I love the word, I act on the word, and I speak the word—Proverbs 18:20.

Storing God's word in my heart is life-changing. I become the word! I become more like Jesus—when I eat of him, my mind, heart, attitude, and behaviour all change. My will begins to line up with God's will. I cannot read God's word and remain the same.

DAY 16

I will not give up when what I see doesn't line up with what I hoped for. If God has given me a vision, a dream, He will bring it to pass. I will keep on watering it with my words of faith. I will continue encouraging others and helping their dreams come to pass. In turn, God will help me too. "What you make happen for others, God will make happen for you," says Mike Murdock. He who refreshes others, he himself will be refreshed—Proverbs 11:25, Galatians 6:7.

DAY 17

I choose to have love in my heart for the poor, the lost and the lonely. I honour God when I show kindness to those in need. I will be blessed by doing what's right when I choose to treat them and love them as I would anyone else. And if I can help with a need, why should I hold back? I choose to walk in love and have compassion on the poor, the lost and the needy—Proverbs 14:21, 31.

DAY 18

How I choose to live makes all the difference; it determines not only the outcome of every situation but also my destiny. I choose to expect that God will meet my every need. A mustard seed takes time to grow, and so do the words of God within my heart, my wisdom and my finances. I will keep on sowing into God's Kingdom because seeds planted do not become full-grown overnight. Proverbs 11 helps me choose to have a wealthy mindset. I am giving generously into the Kingdom of God.

I accept his commands and walk upright and secure. My mouth is a well of life wherever I go, nourishing many. I stand firm through any storm, the Lord is the strength of my life.

DAY 19

I choose to treat everyone with kindness; I have the love and compassion of God in my heart. I have the self-control to rule over my spirit so that the walls of my defences are not broken down. When pressure comes to do wrong or to be unkind, I can remain steady and fixed to God's word and what is right. I can renew my mind with the word of God. When I rule my spirit and have self-control, I can remain steady, calm and stable in any adversity or pressure. I can remain steadfast in my thoughts and emotions. I rely on God's word and His love for me—Proverbs 25:21, 28.

DAY 20

When I am kind and generous to others, I am blessed in return. Whatever I sow, I shall reap and I shall enjoy a sure reward. God does not have to do anything—the reward is inherent within His principles. My ways are pleasant and my path is peace.

I do not crave or envy what the rich man has. He may have gold, but not a heart of gold. I do not wear myself out in pursuit of riches, or even in trying to meet my own needs—God says He will supply my every need and increase my seed sowing and harvest. I have wisdom by putting Him and His Kingdom first in my heart—Proverbs 23:1-8. I honour God with my wealth and my barns shall be full. I am blessed to be a blessing.

DAY 21

I keep close to wisdom and speak wise words, ready to give a wise answer. I treasure God's word; I hunt and seek for wisdom and I shall surely find it. Great rewards are in store for me because I treasure God's word, making it my final authority in life. I will have success in every area of life—Proverbs 2:1-8.

Wisdom is my close companion and daily teacher, even today. Wisdom is my councillor and gives me knowledge, teaching me what is true in a world full of opinions. There is only one truth. Wisdom teaches me what is reliable; I can rely upon the word of God when all other sources and people let me down. God's word gives me the solution and I can give answers to the struggling world.

DAY 22

I walk securely and confidently, trusting and acknowledging God in all my ways. He shall direct my paths. The Lord is my confidence, my firm foundation, my strong tower, and shall keep my foot from being caught in traps and hidden dangers. I choose to fill my thoughts with hope and love and all that is good—Proverbs 3, Philippians 4.

DAY 23

I work well, enjoy the day, and do my best, therefore, my plans shall succeed. I commit my ways fully to Him; He will cause my thoughts to become agreeable to His will. I can expect God to show me His thoughts and His will.

There is a season for everything, so if it appears that nothing is happening, I will keep on sowing and watering because much is happening in the hidden place. When all is quiet, when there is no applause, and when no one sees, God is at work deep within my heart. Immeasurable growth is taking place and my roots of trust are growing stronger.

DAY 24

God is interested in every area of my life—He gives me wisdom and shows me how to look after what He has given me. I choose to be a good steward of what He has given me, and when I am faithful with the little, I can be faithful with much.

DAY 25

I am changing situations and changing the atmosphere. I am altering somebody's day and somebody's life. I am changing my life and populating Heaven, all by my powerful faith-filled, love-filled words.

DAY 26

I am a shining light, a good witness and a good example. I share the love of Jesus wherever I go. I am happy, joyful and peaceful; I am full of life, light and love. I have every blessing, every spiritual gift, and the power to do God's will.

I am alert and active, watching over my word to perform it. The best prayer to offer is to pray God's word back to Him. God is alive and actively performing His word—Jeremiah 1:12.

DAY 27

I allow my words to move me towards what I do want, rather than what I don't want. My words are a God-given powerful tool to succeed, to create, and to change, including my attitude and emotions. If I change what's on the inside, I can change what's on the outside.

I speak life over every fibre of my being—I choose life. I am fit, healthy and strong; I am in the best shape of my life. I have a sharp, clear, and alert mind. I am declaring God's powerful life-changing word over my life.

I am being constantly refreshed. I'm alive, active and productive, and do my work well. I am walking in love and peace and have great opportunities for the Gospel.

DAY 28

When I come upon a problem or temptation and don't know what to do, God's wisdom and guidance will help me because I have His word within on deposit. I have laid up His commandments within me. I am ready for what is next; the Lord is with me and directing me.

I love you Lord—you are my strength, you are my rock, you are my fortress and my deliverer. You are my salvation and in you, I will trust.

DAY 29

God's grace is sufficient for me; His power is made perfect in my weakness. Christ's power may rest on me, for when I am weak, then I am strong. I am asking Big and believing Big because God and His love for me are Big. I am praying, saying, believing and receiving. Hallelujah! If I change what I say, I will change what I see—2Cor. 12:9-10.

DAY 30

I have been delivered from darkness and brought into God's marvellous light. I have the seed of God, and I am filled and sealed with His Holy Spirit. I have been purchased—Jesus paid the price for me, so I am ransomed, healed, and forgiven. I have not been given a spirit of fear, but of love, power, and a sound mind.

"I am Christ's ambassador; I am his mouthpiece and representative on the Earth, telling the good news wherever I go. I am his hands and feet to share the good news, because it is life-changing, eternal good news.

"I AM chosen by God and this is awesome. God, who created the Heavens, the Earth, the galaxies, and the entire universe, chose me. He handpicked me out of all the people living on planet Earth. He mapped out the plan for my life, showing how to get me from where I was to where I am. He knew the exact moment I would be saved, He knew where and when."

"I AM royal, born into a royal family as my Father is the King. He is Lord over every other king, and his Kingdom is unshakeable—it will last forever."

"I AM treasured and special. Out of all the things God could choose for treasure, He chose me."

DAY 31

I set about my work vigorously; my arms are strong for my tasks. My trading is profitable and my lamp does not go out. I open my arms to the poor and extend my hands to the needy. I am clothed with strength and dignity; I can laugh at the days to come. I speak with wisdom and faithful instruction is on my tongue. I watch over the affairs of my household and do not eat the bread of idleness. My children arise and call me blessed.

Charm is deceptive and beauty is fleeting, but someone who fears the Lord is to be praised. I am happy, healthy, and purposeful. I speak what I believe and believe what I speak. I am blessed to be a blessing; I have extraordinary opportunities given to me—Proverbs 31.

15

MY NEW NAME

My old name was Depressed, my new name is Joy
My old name was Worry, my new name is Trust
My old name was Fear, my new name is Love
My old name was Pride, my new name is Humility

My old name was Pitiful, my new name is Powerful
My old name was Negativity, my new name is Positivity
My old name was Weary, my new name is Energy
My old name was Misery, my new name is Life

CLOSING WORDS

The power of our words shapes our lives, so it is easy for us to make messes of our lives. We can also speak beautiful, clean, and tidy over something ugly, dirty, and messy. We speak life and blessings instead of what our eyes can see. We realize nothing is about ourselves, but obedience to God and His plan. Live this day with passion and on purpose, surrendered to His will. Be a life-changer; tell the good news of Jesus wherever you go. Choose to look to him who is love. He can do more than you could ever think, ask, or imagine. With all that you are, praise the Lord always.

QUOTES

CHAPTER 2

Mike Murdock, "What you make happen for others, God will make happen for you."

Edward Mote, Hymn. "My hope is build on nothing less than Jesus Christ my righteousness." "On Christ the solid rock I stand, all other ground is sinking sand."

CHAPTER 7

Don Fransico, "Praise the Lord Hallelu, I don't care what the devil's gonna do, my word in faith is my sword and shield. Jesus is the Lord of the way I feel."

CHAPTER 11

Henry Ford, "Whether you think you can, or you think you can't – you're right."

CHAPTER 12

Derek Prince, 'The divine exchange.' "Believing and thanking, thanking and believing, are like a spiral staircase that will take you continually higher into the fullness of God's provision."

ABOUT THE AUTHOR

Lesley Ann Whittle is an author, speaker and bible teacher who helps individuals find truth and freedom so they can become all that God created them to be. For over ten years she has helped Reverend Michael K Whittle pastor Good News Gospel Church. Together they have worked at the Amazing Charity Shop, changing lives in the UK and overseas by raising funds to build schools and water wells, and support community centres and orphanages in Uganda, India and Pakistan. Lesley lives in the UK and has two sons and two grandsons. Connect at lesleyannwhittle.com.

BATTLEFIELD OF
THE HEART
EXPERIENCE

www.lesleyannwhittle.com

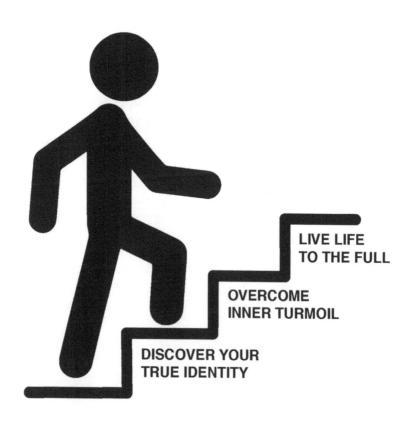

LIVE LIFE
TO THE FULL

OVERCOME
INNER TURMOIL

DISCOVER YOUR
TRUE IDENTITY

Lightning Source UK Ltd.
Milton Keynes UK
UKHW022231240920
370471UK00010B/365

9 781647 463656